THE LAST WILD HORSE

Heads up, alert for possible danger, Przhevalsky horses looked like this when they roamed freely on the open ranges of Europe and Asia. Heavy winter coats let them ignore the snow on trees and ground. Today they can be seen only in zoos, as here at Hellabrunn in Munich, West Germany.

THE
LAST
WILD
HORSE

BY MORRIS WEEKS

Houghton Mifflin Company Boston 1977

We are grateful to the following sources for permission to include photographs in this book: the photographs on pages 28, 35, and 43 courtesy of The American Museum of Natural History; Toni Angermayer, Photo Researchers, Inc., for the photographs on pages ii and 23; The Bettmann Archive, Inc., for the photographs on pages 78 and 97; Irene Brady for the drawing on page 40 from *America's Horses and Ponies* (Houghton Mifflin Company); Ron Garrison, San Diego Zoo, for the photographs on pages 8 and 16; Carl Hagenbeck's Zoo for the photographs on pages 73, 106, and 108; Mary Littauer for the photograph on page 119; F. D. Schmidt, San Diego Zoo, for the photographs on pages 12 and 14; Dr. Jiří Volf for the photographs on pages 3, 22, and 130; The Zoological Garden (Prague), Dr. Jiří Volf, editor, for the reproduction from the Przhevalsky studbook on page 123; and The Zoological Institute, USSR Academy of Sciences, for the photograph on page 58.

Maps on pages 37, 63, 70, and 131 by Linda Sturgis.

Library of Congress Cataloging in Publication Data
Weeks, Morris.
   The last wild horse.

   Bibliography: p.
   SUMMARY: A biography of the Russian explorer who discovered a species of wild horse in Mongolia. Also discusses several attempts by zookeepers to breed these horses in captivity.
     1. Equus przewalskii—Juvenile literature. 2. Przhevalskii, Nikolai Mikhailovich, 1839–1888—Juvenile literature. 3. Explorers—Russia—Biography—Juvenile literature. [1. Przhevalskii, Nikolai Mikhailovich, 1839–1888. 2. Explorers. 3. Przhevalski's horse. 4. Horses] I. Title.
   QL737.U62W43   599'.725 [92]   77-13392

Library of Congress Cataloging in Publication Data
ISBN 0-395-25838-3

TO TONY
who was looking for something else
in the encyclopedia

FOREWORD

To write a book about a wild horse, it helps to know at least one tame horse. Being close to a domestic horse for any length of time makes you appreciate its looks and qualities, the way it stands and runs and comes to nibble your hand, its grace, strength, and individual charm. With that background, you can't help being attracted to the horse's wild "cousin" when you see one.

That's how it was with me. I met my first tame horse by being hoisted onto his back and told to go ahead, ride him. I didn't think he was so darned tame. In fact, I promptly fell off. But I survived to try again and eventually learned to ride, and so was born a lifelong friendship between horses and me.

The first tame horse entered my life in a small town in California. Some years later and thousands of miles eastward, while my wife and I were vacationing in Europe, I met my first wild horse at a zoo. Up to that moment I hadn't known that the wild horse existed. But because I liked domestic ones, I naturally wanted to know more about this strange animal with the almost unpronounceable name of *Equus przewalskii*.

The wild horse, I learned, is something special. Quite possibly the living ancestor of the domestic horse, it was thought to be extinct until it was discovered somewhere in Asia by "the famous Russian explorer Przhevalsky." Famous? I'd never heard of him. So I began asking questions: Who was Przhevalsky? What was he doing in Asia? Just what kind of horse did he find? How come someone else didn't find it sooner? The more answers I got, the more questions I asked. Finally, I felt I knew the unique story of *Equus przewalskii* well enough to try to share it with others.

Putting this book together took a lot of reading, considerable traveling, quite a few interviews, and reams of notes. I was lucky to have access to the best source book on the Przhevalsky horse, Dr. Erna Mohr's *The Asiatic Wild Horse*, along with two other books recently published in England, Dr. Sándor Bökönyi's *The Prjevalsky Horse* and Donald Rayfield's *The Dream of Lhasa*. These books and others that I consulted are listed in the bibliography.

I also had personal help. Dr. Jiří Volf of the Prague Zoo in Czechoslovakia, Dr. Heinz Heck of the Catskill Game Farm, and Curator James G. Doherty of the New York Zoological Park supplied much useful information. In particular I must thank Vladimir and Mary Littauer, a couple known to many horse lovers. Russian-born Vladimir, a longtime United States resident, has written a dozen books on equitation. Mary, his American wife, is a student of many subjects, including such unusual ones as the saddles, bridles, chariots, and other gear used with horses thousands of years ago. The Littauers lent me books, translated articles for me, and gave unstintingly of their specialized knowledge.

I hope the result is interesting reading and that the book may contribute a little to the argument over keeping wild animals alive in the world, just as *Equus przewalskii* has been kept alive — so far.

Morris Weeks, Jr.

THE LAST WILD HORSE

THE HORSE

The keeper quietly opens the gate and walks into the sunlit enclosure. Surrounded by heavy wire fencing, it is nearly half the size of a football field. It is empty except for a small feeding shed, where hay lies on the ground, some big wooden water tubs nearby, and a chunky, powerfully built animal that watches him steadily from about forty feet away.

The animal is a classic example of the Przhevalsky or Mongolian horse, sometimes called the "ancestor of the domestic horse," and it is one of the last wild horses left on earth. Hunted and starved to almost certain extinction in its native Asia, the Przhevalsky (the approximate Russian pronunciation is Przh - VAHL - skee) may yet be

1

snatched from the brink of final disappearance by planned breeding in a few special zoos around the world. The Catskill Game Farm in upstate New York is such a zoo.

This particular horse, Rolox, son of a stallion named Rolo and a mare named Roxie, is three years old, weighs close to 500 pounds, and could split the keeper's skull with one well-placed kick. In another year or so, he will be ready to become a breeding stallion himself, at the Catskill Game Farm or at some other zoo.

His sleek summer coat is a light dun, almost the shade of pale honey, setting off a black mane and a long black tail. The mane stands up stiffly, like a brush a good six inches long, with no forelock between the ears, and the upper part of the tail is covered with short, light-colored hairs. The neck and chest are solid, even massive, and the jaw muscles bulge. His nose is beige gray, as though he had just dipped it in flour, and the same pale color rims his large brown eyes. Black hairs edge his ears, inside and out. Perhaps because of his deep, thick neck, Rolox's head doesn't seem quite in scale with the rest of him.

A brown stripe runs the length of his back and vanishes in his tail hairs. His legs are black up to the knee joint; above that, on the forelegs, are horizontal brown markings almost like a zebra's stripes. The yellowish tone of his body shades down to near-white under the belly.

Notable Przhevalsky characteristics—muscular body, heavy head, brushlike mane, light areas on nose and belly, dark lower legs—appear on a stallion named Bars, photographed at the zoo in Prague, Czechoslovakia.

The keeper says with some pride that Rolox shows nearly perfect Przhevalsky characteristics. "Colors, markings, length of tail — they vary from one individual to the next. Some Przhevalskys are almost gray, some almost red brown. And so on. But if you wanted all the ideal Przhevalsky features in one animal, Rolox would be about as close as you could get.

"There's another distinctive quality in this horse apart from his looks. He's — how can I say it? —

aloof. He draws an invisible line between himself and the human race, maybe twenty feet or so from wherever he happens to be, and he'll never cross that line unless he's been drugged to unconsciousness. He's a wild animal all the way.

"A few Przhevalskys, usually mares, get so used to people that they'll let you pat their necks or rub their noses. They might take sugar from your hand. I've read of Przhevalskys, in Europe, that were saddled and ridden. But not Rolox. You couldn't put a rope on him, much less a saddle."

The keeper tosses an apple gently toward Rolox. It stops about twenty feet away. The horse shies and whirls, trots off a few steps, then turns back: He has caught the sweet fruit scent. Eyes riveted on the man, he moves slowly forward. Suddenly, his natural wariness takes over and he breaks away, snorting, forefeet pawing, to vanish behind the shed.

The keeper doesn't move — and a moment later Rolox reappears and again starts toward the apple. Twice he stops, snorts, and decides to keep trying. He stalks the apple. Step by slow step, nostrils wide, eyes never leaving the keeper, he draws nearer. His long upper lip touches the fruit, and in a golden blur of movement he takes it in his mouth, swivels away on all four feet, and shoots at a full gallop to the far end of the enclosure.

"In the wild," the keeper says, "they can run like that for hours. *Could* run, that is. Maybe one or two will still be sighted in the desert somewhere, but how long can a few individuals hold out? For all practical purposes the wild Przhevalsky is finished. You can't even call it an endangered species anymore — not if all the wild ones are dead. The only way to save this magnificent animal was by putting it in zoos."

Is the Przhevalsky horse worth the effort to save it? That may be hard to answer without knowing more about the animal. To start with, where did it get that strange-looking name?

The name is Russian, which is one reason why it looks strange — to non-Russians, anyway. The Russian alphabet differs from ours, and some Russian sounds can't be rendered accurately in our letters. Different people have tried to spell this particular name in a number of ways, from Przhevalsky, Prjevalsky, and Przewalski to Przheval'skiy and still other forms. It also appears in the possessive, as "Przhevalsky's" and so on. For consistency, this book sticks with "Przhevalsky."

Other names for the wild horse are used in its native Asia. The Mongol word is *takhi*. The Kirghiz people of Russia and western China call it *kurtag*. Both of these names, too, may turn up in different spellings.

The scientific name, however, being in Latin, is always the same: *Equus przewalskii* Poliakov. *Equus,* of course, means horse. Then come the names of two men. The first, Nicolai Mikhailovich Przhevalsky, was the Russian explorer who obtained the hide and skull of an unknown animal in central Asia in 1878. The second, I. S. Poliakov (PAUL-yah-koff), was the St. Petersburg zoologist who identified the remains as those of a true wild horse. Both these men will appear later in the book.

Not all zoologists agree that the Przhevalsky horse should be called *Equus przewalskii* rather than *Equus caballus*, the name given to domestic horses. The different name means that the Przhevalsky is considered a separate species. Some zoologists think it is; others don't. Both animals are descended from the same wild ancestor, and they may have more points of similarity than of difference. Still, *Equus przewalskii* is distinct enough from *Equus caballus* to be called a different animal by most zoologists.

Many people think a wild horse is one that has escaped from captivity or is the descendant of one. Not so. Though such horses may indeed run free on the open range — in Nevada, say, or on Chincoteague, the island off Virginia that "Misty" made famous — their direct kinship with other domestic horses is unmistakable. They are properly called *feral*, as is any domestic animal that has taken up life in the wild.

A true wild animal is one whose ancestors have never been domesticated, never tamed. It differs more or less from the domestic form in the ways it looks, thinks, and acts, even as a wolf differs from a dog. Seen in this light, the Przhevalsky is definitely not *Equus caballus*, but is truly the last wild horse in the world.

There still is a lot we don't know about the Przhevalsky horse. While domestic horses have been around for thousands of years, the wild ones — which date back *millions* of years — were discovered, or rediscovered, only a century ago in the remote, rugged mountains and deserts of Mongolia (between Siberia and China) and the neighboring area of Sinkiang in northwestern China. Even there they were growing scarce and hard to find, much less study. Pursued by native tribesmen, cut off from many former sources of food and water, they had become extremely shy. Przhevalsky himself writes of managing to get close to one small herd — "but suddenly one of the animals noticed me. At once they galloped away at the top of their speed and vanished from my sight."

Later travelers observed and made notes on the horses, and a few trained zoologists have penetrated their forbidding terrain. From the sightings they made, and the experience of Mongolians and Chinese with the animals, comes a sketchy but probably accurate picture of the Przhevalsky "lifestyle." It may have disappeared now, but we will speak of it in the present tense.

Wild Przhevalskys live in small groups or herds.

This is a representative Przhevalsky mare. Compared to stallions, the mares are normally smaller, lighter, and less thick in neck and chest.

A group normally consists of a mature stallion with several mares and the young horses or recent foals that he has sired. Young horses divide about evenly between males and females, but when the males are old enough, about three years old, the leader forces them out to fend for themselves. Eventually, with luck, they will form herds of their own.

The fillies (young females) stay with the group into which they were born. But as they grow older they may be led or chased away by a strange stallion, even one from the original group. The same may happen with mature mares. If a strange stallion does not actually approach one, she may leave the herd anyway and join him. The original stallion will fight to prevent this as long as he can, but sooner or later there will be some regrouping.

So long as the head of a herd maintains his position, he is the group's leader, protector, and absolute boss. He alone decides when and where the herd will graze, drink, rest, or move on. Wild horses generally travel in single file. When danger threatens, the mares and young animals line up with a young stallion at their head while the mature leader guards the rear. Any animal who ignores the leader's wishes at any time will be shoved, kicked, or, if necessary, bitten into obedience.

The presence of humans has greatly affected the behavior of the wild horses. Generally, they graze and seek water at night, resting in some secluded spot by day.

Their diet is a matter of necessity, not choice. They would prefer good grass, but they have been pushed into semidesert where the main vegetation is coarse, tough plants that can grow in salty soil. The horses have to survive on such things as saxaul (a leafless shrub that grows as high as fifteen feet), tamarisk, wormwood, feathergrass, rhubarb roots, and the bulbs of wild tulips. In some sandy expanses the only plant is a low bush that forms isolated tufts. Even this scant fodder may be hard to find, forcing the animals to keep moving to avoid starvation.

Drinking water is even more scarce. The Przhevalsky can go up to three days without it, four in a pinch, but water holes are not common in central Asia and human beings have preempted most of them.

Every wild horse has instincts about predators — tigers, lions, leopards — that can spring from ambush, land on a horse's back with crushing force, and kill with a single bite. (This may be why even a domestic horse rears and bucks the first time anything strange touches its back.) Today the big cats are gone from the Przhevalsky's range and its main natural enemies are wolves and bears. A wild stallion in good condition can handle either one. Mares protecting their young are also dangerous fighters.

When Mongolian tribesmen wanted to catch wild horses to add to their domestic herds, or for zoos, they normally left the adults strictly alone and concentrated on the foals. By following them continuously on horseback, changing to fresh mounts as needed, the riders could tire the young animals to the point where they dropped out of the herd and could be captured with a rope lasso on the end of a long stick. Humans, the Przhevalsky has learned, are one enemy that can be neither defeated nor outwitted.

A Przhevalsky horse transported from the open

range to confinement in a zoo starts its new life in uncertainty and fear. These feelings lessen as the animal grows used to its surroundings but may never really disappear. Foals adjust more easily than mares and mares are more tractable than stallions. Some stallions remain totally untamable.

No wild horse has been captured in years, but scores have been born in captivity. These start life in the only environment they will ever know. Nevertheless, they behave much as they would if they were still in the wild — at least for several generations.

If a zoo lacks room for even a small breeding herd and simply puts one or two horses on display, they usually are given just about enough space to eat and sleep in. But, with adequate quarters, the Przhevalskys follow their established patterns. Stallions form herds, mares guard their young, and immature stallions leave the herd when the time comes. This is their natural way. From the breeder's point of view, it also is the best way to keep the horses healthy.

Though a Przhevalsky herd is in effect an "extended family," it enjoys little of what we would call family life. The head stallion may not attack his children, as some animal fathers do, but neither does he play with them as others will. Rather, he tolerates them. He may show playful "courtship" behavior toward a mare before mating but at other times he is more domineering than affectionate.

The Catskill Game Farm keeper recalls a time when one stallion spent two days and nights patrolling his herd to make sure none of the members ate or drank. Why? "Guess he didn't think it was safe." Was it? "Of course. But go tell that to a stallion."

Mares in the zoo herd usually get along together and may form lasting friendships. But their main concern is for their foals. Przhevalsky mares are ready for mating at from three to five years of age, the stallions at a year or so later. Both sexes may remain fertile into their twenties. Individuals of both sexes have lived in captivity past the age of thirty. One mare, the oldest on record as this is written, died in the Cincinnati Zoo at thirty-four.

A pregnant mare carries her foal about eleven months on average. Records kept at the zoo in Prague, Czechoslovakia (a world breeding center for Przhevalskys), show that most foals are born in late spring and early summer. When the time to give birth is about two weeks off, the mare begins to look for a place where she can be by herself, away from the rest of the herd. A well-run zoo provides a separate area for this purpose, with a private shelter and straw for the mother to lie on.

The birth itself normally takes only a few minutes. (One zookeeper who wanted to witness the event missed it because moments beforehand he

At left. Przhevalskys on the run: two young fillies in sleek summer coats kick up the dust as they race with others in the San Diego Wild Animal Park.

had to go answer the telephone.) The newborn foal is an awkward little creature, long-legged and wobbly, with a light coat and tufts of curly hair along its neck. But it starts running about in a matter of hours and plays with its mother and the other foals within its first week. Its coat gradually darkens, and

Young and trusting—for a wild animal—this foal shows baby features, including the fuzzy mane and short tail, but the pale nose and dark lower portions of the legs help establish her as a true Przhevalsky.

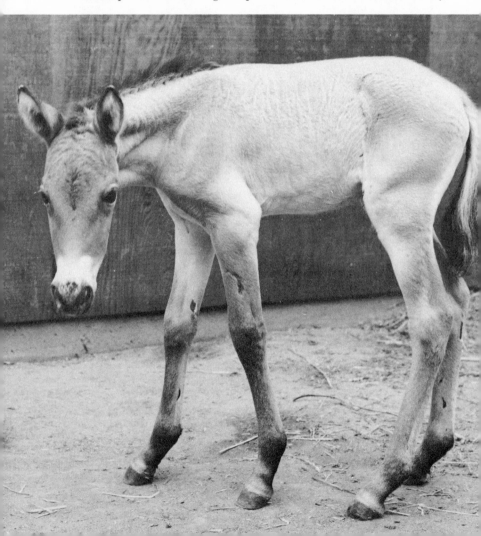

at about six months its true mane grows in.

Given the opportunity, a foal stays with its mother until it is two years or more old. During that time, it may frolic like a puppy with others its own age. Young stallions and fillies show a happy capacity for play — rearing, pretending to kick or bite, racing about, sliding to sudden stops — that older horses seem to forget.

If a zoo wants its Przhevalskys to breed regularly, it can change the usual pattern of mother-foal association. For example, the New York Zoological Park (commonly called the Bronx Zoo) tries to mate a breeding mare as soon as possible after she has given birth. This normally can be done in about three weeks. Thus the earlier foal is in the yearling stage when its mother is ready to produce another baby. At that point she and the yearling are separated — permanently.

"The mare goes into an isolation stall," explains a zoo curator, "and the yearling is put in with the rest of the Przhevalsky herd. That's its first such experience, and it can be traumatic for a day or two. It can't see its mother anymore, but they call back and forth to each other. Then, sooner than you might think, they both accept the situation. By the time the new foal is born, the yearling has been on its own a while and has learned to like being independent.

"This system has another plus. A mare with a newborn foal is extremely protective. She will kick

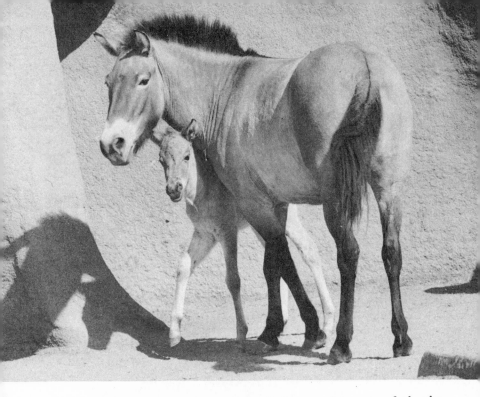

A Przhevalsky mare looms protectively over her young foal, who peers out curiously. The foal's legs are almost as long as its mother's, but its head and body will take years to reach full adult size.

any other horse that comes too near, including her own yearling. So we may have saved several yearlings some unnecessary pain — or even broken bones."

The mares and young animals in a herd lead generally relaxed lives, but the head stallion is under constant psychological pressure. His day-to-day job, as he sees it, is to protect his herd, and he devotes a lot of time and energy to it. A study at one zoo showed the Przhevalsky mares moving about actively for only a little over an hour and a half a day,

16

while the stallion was active for more than four hours. (The rest of the time presumably was occupied by eating, sleeping, and socializing.)

The stallion regards anything outside his own group — even a familiar keeper, source of food and water — as a menace. One European zoo reports that its Przhevalsky stallions may attack not only people but cars. At another zoo, where the grounds are spacious, one stallion spent much of his time pacing round and round his herd. This had its good side, the zoo director noted. The animals were kept from getting near the public, so "the foals are not ruined by being constantly fed sugar."

Unfortunately, no one can predict just how a wild stallion will behave. The Bronx Zoo had one named Bert who started out as one of the most pleasant animals anyone could want. "For months he came and went quietly with the rest of the herd, behaved like a perfect gentleman. The same keeper fed him and took care of him the whole time. But one day, when the keeper wasn't looking, Bert came up and bit him hard in the back. Then he kicked him. The keeper was hurt, all right, but he got over that. What really hurt was the change in an animal he'd come to love.

"Yes, Bert is still with us. But no one tries to get anywhere near him any more."

A stallion guarding his herd usually keeps it up even at feeding time. The others eat and drink in order — mares with foals first, then mares without foals and any young animals in the group. Finally the stallion, who has been on watch until the others finish, takes his turn — with one eye still out for danger.

Feeding policy varies from zoo to zoo, but the basic element in all Przhevalsky diets is hay. Hay and grass need considerable chewing, which is essential to help preserve the powerful jaw muscles. Grain also is a staple, often a mixture of oats, corn, and so on. This may be prepared in the zoo or bought from outside suppliers, loosely mixed or pressed in the form of cakes or pellets. Green grass is welcomed by the horses when they can get it. (The Bronx Zoo makes it available all year by growing it hydroponically, in nutrient-rich water.) Vitamin and mineral supplements are added to the diet as seems desirable. Typically, these supplements are the same as those recommended for domestic horses and come from commercial sources.

Whatever the diet, most zoos feed it impartially to all their wild horses, though some may add more vitamins and minerals for pregnant mares and animals that are ailing or getting old. A new foal, of course, like other mammal babies, is nourished by its mother's milk. But it starts tasting adult food in a month or so, gradually making the transition from an all milk diet to an all hay-and-grain one.

Like many other animals, wild horses, even in small groups, sort themselves out according to what

18

may be an instinctive social system. As if by common agreement, some individuals dominate others, and all respect the arrangement. The head stallion is undisputed Number One. Then comes the leading mare, who outranks the other mares. She wins her position by assuming it, if she can, by fighting for it, if she must — mares fight with a great show of teeth, but actually by kicking — and then she has to maintain it against challenges from other mares.

The leading mare's position is a potential source of trouble if she and other mares in the herd are pregnant at the same time. Then the stallion must be taken away from the group because, while the other mares probably would not object to his presence, the leading mare might decide that he threatened her rank and could start a fight with him. That could damage both horses and even result in a dead foal.

Separating the animals in such situations can be termed preventive medicine. So is the common practice of worming foals (just as puppies are wormed) when they start nibbling at adult food that may be contaminated by other animals' droppings. If a horse gets an infection or is hurt in an accident or a fight, however, the zoo veterinarian is called in. He or she may decide that the injury will heal itself, perhaps helped along by antibiotics. If need be, the animal is kept by itself until it returns to health.

Mares and young horses usually can be treated for minor ailments without creating problems. Attention to matters requiring more handling — and indeed all matters involving stallions — may call for a tranquilizer to calm the animal, or an anesthetic to put it out. Various kinds are available. One widely used is called M-99 and is administered with a hypodermic needle like the ones used for people (though it's bigger and carries a larger dose).

If the horse is in a small enclosure and can be reached through the fence, a quick poke by the vet does the trick. If that is not practical, the standard device is the Cap-Chur Gun — a kind of pistol powered by carbon dioxide that shoots a dart loaded with the desired drug. The gun is accurate up to about fifteen feet away. Once the dart pricks the animal's skin, the horse goes down almost instantly for as long as necessary (the time is controlled by the dosage). Then the vet trims the hooves, works on the teeth, dresses the wound, or whatever. When he or she is finished, an antidote may be given to wake the horse up, steady it on its feet, and control possible side effects from the original drug. (The antidote for M-99 also can be injected to save a human being if a dart flies wild and pricks someone by mistake. Otherwise the person will be dead in approximately one minute. To date this has not been reported anywhere.)

Wild horses, like many other animals in captivity, tend to grow bored by the lack of variety in their daily lives. Various ways to lessen boredom have been found useful. One is simplicity itself: feeding skys in captivity seem indifferent to cold weather. When many other animals seek heated shelters, the horses stay outdoors and thrive, pawing snow away from their hay and relishing water that freezes over at night. Zoos in warmer climates, incidentally, find that the horses' winter coats tend not to grow so long and dense as they do in colder areas.

Changes in the way wild animals look and act usually appear after a few generations in captivity. Przhevalskys in zoos tend to grow more like domestic horses with time. Their behavior is much the same to start with, at least superficially. For example, the Przhevalsky neighs or whinnies (a whinny

Social (and sociable) behavior: two Przhevalskys stand side-by-side to help each other get ready for summer by biting out itchy winter hairs.

is a gentle neigh) in the same way and for the same reasons as does a domestic horse — that is, when it is expecting food or water, or because it scents another horse.

On the other hand, domestic horses don't shed their mane and tail hairs on an annual basis. (Like people, they lose and replace one hair at a time.) Nor do they fight like Przhevalskys.

A fight between two Przhevalsky stallions is a violent spectacle. Ears flat back, teeth bared, eyes blazing, either may attack without warning. Or each of them may take a peculiarly menacing posture with neck stretched forward, head so low the under-lip nearly touches the ground and eyes squint upward like some kind of demon. In this position the two circle each other in what has been described as a "slinking walk." Suddenly, they rush at each other. Each tries to catch the other by the nape of the neck with his teeth; with a good grip, he can throw his opponent to the ground. Kicking and biting savagely, he can inflict serious damage or even kill the other horse.

Domestic stallions also fight. Those who have escaped and gone feral can be fierce indeed. But, on the evidence, a feral stallion is no match for a Przhevalsky. This is attested to by witnesses in Mongolia, where domestic animals wander off now and then from carelessly watched herds. If a stallion and his mares go feral, it is sure to interest any Przhevalsky stallion in the neighborhood.

It happened once, in 1952, with recorded results. Some feral horses encountered a lone wild stallion. The feral stallion began a fight to protect the mares. Later, the feral stallion's body was found with its legs broken, ears ripped off, and chunks of skin and flesh gouged out. And the Przhevalsky had taken over the herd.

Scientists have found some other interesting differences between wild and domestic horses. For example, while the number of vertebrae in the spine is always the same in normal domestic horses, half of the Przhevalskys in one study proved to have an extra vertebra in the chest section, hence an extra pair of ribs. This might indicate a mutation — a sudden evolutionary change — in those individuals. Or it might mean that the skeletons of a good many Przhevalskys have not evolved as fully as the skeletons of domestic horses.

A more complex type of research concerns chromosomes. Chromosomes are the tiny bodies in the nuclei of living cells that contain the genes, which in turn transmit all the hereditary traits, from color of hair to shape of toes, that are passed from parent to offspring. In all higher mammals the chromosomes in each cell nucleus are arranged in sets of two. It has been shown that chromosomes tend to become larger and fewer as a species evolves. Since the domestic horse has sixty-four chromosomes (thirty-two sets), people thought the

Przhevalsky might have more than that if it were indeed a less evolved animal. Sure enough, recent tests on a limited number of Przhevalskys showed a chromosome count of sixty-six for each one.

Surprisingly, this chromosome difference does not affect the ability of wild and domestic horses to interbreed and have fertile offspring. Domestic horses and donkeys can interbreed despite unlike chromosome counts (sixty-four and sixty-two respectively), but they produce only mules (donkey father, horse mother) or hinnies (horse father, donkey mother), both of which usually are sterile. A mule or hinny is the last of its very short line. But the offspring of Przhevalsky–domestic horse matings have been bred with other crossbred animals as well as wild and domestic horses. This situation, as we will see, has led to arguments about the purity of alleged Przhevalsky horses in certain zoos.

Counting chromosomes is a specialized skill and interpreting the results is even more so. Much work remains to be done. One researcher believes that the chromosome count can become a major tool in establishing the true ancestry of any individual animal. In time it may well help to answer many other questions.

Wild or domestic, all horses are classified zoologically in the family of *Equidae* or equids. This includes all living forms and their ancestors back for some 60 million years, one of the longest known "family trees" of any mammal on earth. The living members of the family make up the genus *Equus*, with four subgenera. One subgenus is the horse. The other three are the zebras, native to Africa; the true wild asses, also African and ancestors of the domestic donkey; and the so-called wild asses of Asia, including the onagers, kiangs, and kulans, all of which show some characteristics of both asses and horses.* Today every *Equus* subgenus is endangered in the wild, though none so much as the Przhevalsky horse.

The family of *Equidae* is one of three in the order of perissodactyls (that is, mammals having an odd number of toes on the hind foot). The other two families in the order are the rhinoceroses and the tapirs. They have three toes on each hind foot. The equids have a single toe on all four feet — or, more precisely, a hoof — which has evolved from the nail on what once was the equid's middle toe.

The difference between a tiny toenail and a big, solid, hornlike hoof is one measure of how long the evolution of the equids has taken and how very slowly the changes in structure must have occurred. Over time, the process has transformed a creature no bigger than a fox (and a lot less smart) into the modern horse. The equid record includes twists and turns, offshoots and blind alleys. At least nineteen

---

*In contrast to horses, wild asses tend to form female herds with female leaders, while zebras usually mingle the sexes in herds with no apparent leaders.

genera of equids developed, flourished, and died out by the time the final genus *Equus* was established.

Going back even farther, humans and equids once had a common ancestor. Close to 100 million years ago when the dinosaurs were dying out, the first mammals and birds appeared. These early mammals were simple, generalized creatures that needed to make up their minds (or have the environment do it for them) whether they would be-

Sixty million years of evolution are dramatized in this museum exhibit. From the tiny *Eohippus* (reconstructed), the growth of the horse led at last to the modern *Equus*, whose skeleton dwarfs its ancient ancestor.

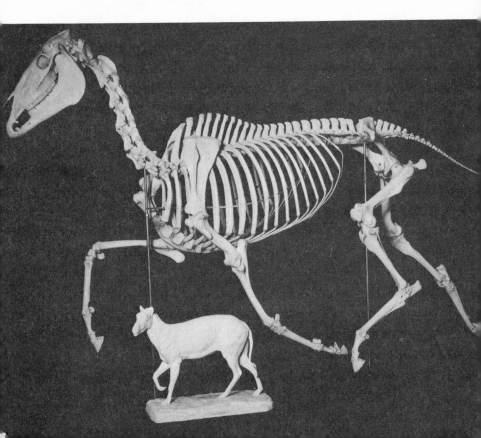

come herbivores or carnivores, live on land or in water, form groups or go it alone. By the time this state of undifferentiátion was resolved, the animals that eventually would become *Homo sapiens* had divided from those destined to lead to *Equus*.

The first appearance of human beings was still far in the future when the ancestor of all the equids — and of all the hoofed mammals we know today, from antelopes to elephants — came on the scene. This was the condylarth, a small creature with a long, low body and an arched back, a long and heavy tail, a primitive skull with the eyes midway between nose and ears, and a tiny brain. It had five toes on each foot. On each toe was a little hoof, pointing the way for every equid.

Condylarths helped usher in what geologists call the Cenozoic era, a time span that began roughly 75 million years ago and runs up to the present moment. The Cenozoic sometimes is called the Age of Mammals. Most geologists divide it into seven epochs, about like this:

Epoch	*Approximate time span*
Recent	25,000 years ago to present
Pleistocene	2 million to 25,000 years ago
Pliocene	10 to 2 million years ago
Miocene	25 to 10 million years ago
Oligocene	35 to 25 million years ago

| Eocene | 55 to 35 million years ago |
| Paleocene | 75 to 55 million years ago |

Reading from bottom to top, equid evolution crosses all seven epochs and can be clearly traced in the increasing size and complexity of fossil remains from each successive epoch.

The tracing of equid remains began in 1838 — though no one knew it at the time. An English naturalist named William Richardson was looking for fossil plants on the coast of Kent, south of London. Finding some, he decided to look further, and came on the skull of a small animal with most of the teeth intact. He didn't know what to make of it. The following year, another Englishman, Richard Owen, concluded that it looked like the skull of a living African mammal, the rabbitlike hyrax. He named it *Hyracotherium*.

Geology still was a young science then, but people were beginning to look for fossil skulls and bones in England, France, and other parts of Europe. When enough had been turned up, it occurred to the diggers that some bones bore a sort of familial relationship to others. Then, in 1859, Charles Darwin published his remarkable book *On the Origin of Species*. In it he offered strong arguments that life on earth has evolved in response to changes in environmental conditions — climate, food supply, and the like. Soon the geologists saw that many "related" fossils had more than a resemblance: they were successive stages in the evolution of various animals.

Now for the first time European equid fossils were arranged in order of age. And it became evident that the oldest of them all was *Hyracotherium*. Far from being some kind of hyrax, it actually was (and still is) the earliest known horse.

Not much larger than a fox, *Hyracotherium* probably looked a lot like its ancestor, the condylarth. But the needs of its way of life had already reduced the number of its toes to four in front and three in back, with the middle toes bearing most of the weight. Its teeth had changed, too. A condylarth might have eaten just about anything, but *Hyracotherium's* teeth were clearly those of a herbivore.

This animal evolved further over the next few million years, but its descendants finally became extinct in Europe. Meanwhile, it, or an equid almost exactly like it, had appeared in America.

The existence of this animal in the Western Hemisphere bears out a theory: Many geologists believe that Europe and the Americas originally lay close together, with land connections over which animals could pass in both directions. Gradually, the continents drifted apart. About 45 million years ago the connections vanished. But when *Hyracotherium* fossils were first found in America, they were not recognized as such and the name *Eohippus* or "Dawn Horse," the horse of the Eocene epoch, was given to the tiny equid. Specialists still prefer the original name.

Equid evolution in the New World from *Eohippus* to today's *Equus*, along with the many side branches that in some cases lasted millions of years before dying out, has been traced through fossils found plentifully in western North America, particularly in a broad band running from Texas north to Canada. In this area, countless equids lived and died during the long, slow passage of the epochs. Their bones mostly were absorbed into the soil. Some, though, were preserved in muddy or sandy deposits that eventually were buried under other deposits and finally transformed into rock. The bones lay there until, much, much later, erosion exposed them to view. That happened most often in sandstone and other relatively soft beds, the kind that have formed such colorful sights as the Bad Lands of South Dakota and the Painted Desert of Arizona.

The men and women who use fossils to reconstruct the lives of extinct animals and plants are called paleontologists. For the last century or so they have combed the spots where equid fossils show up.

A paleontologists's job is not easy. He or she may have to spend months in the outdoors, sun-baked and rain-drenched, looking for bits of bone on the ground or for evidence that bones may be found by digging. Often enough, digging yields nothing. And if bone fragments are found embedded in rock or soil (as they usually are), the latter must be chipped, picked, or blown away by hand. Then the fragments must go to a laboratory to be pieced together, compared centimeter by centimeter with other fossils, and, finally, identified as known genera or species whose age can be stated — or set aside as still among the unknown.

The paleontologist's reward for all this is the personal satisfaction of adding to human knowledge (plus, of course, the recognition he or she gains among other scientists). For the rest of us, such largely unsung efforts have produced a striking record of equid evolution.

Thus, we know that the Eocene horse lived in North America during a lengthy period when much of the continent was warm and swampy, with thick semitropical forests. *Eohippus* (or *Hyracotherium*) was a browser, an eater of leaves. Slowly the climate changed. Steady warmth gave way to seasonal variations — now warmer, now cooler. The forests gave way to open areas that grew into grassy plains. All animals responded to these environmental changes by moving elsewhere, dying out, or evolving.

The Eocene horse evolved markedly by the time the Eocene passed into the Oligocene, so much so that the horse of the latter epoch has a different name, *Mesohippus*. Over some 20 million years its teeth became much like those of today's *Equus*. The modern horse has relatively short front teeth, used

33

mainly for taking in food (and biting), while its cheek teeth, the ones it chews with, are longer, stronger, and armored with hard enamel and cement. As the tooth surface wears away with use, new surface is produced by the growth of bone under the teeth. This lets the horse eat any green thing it fancies: grass, hay, grain, leaves, fruit, even small branches. *Mesohippus*, descendant of browsers, was beginning to eat the same kind of food today's horse eats.

Mesohippus showed other changes. To permit grazing along with browsing, its head and neck grew longer. To see better in open country, it grew taller — though still small, no more than two feet at the shoulder. To help it run from pursuers, its feet developed. Each foot had only three toes, with the side toes touching the ground only lightly. All these developments continued in the late Oligocene when we find a new equid — the larger, stronger, and faster *Miohippus*.

The horse of the next epoch, the Miocene, is called *Merychippus*. This is the first equid that is known, from its tooth structure, to have given up browsing for good. It must have lived almost entirely in open country and depended for safety on speed of foot. Its two small side toes no longer touched the ground except when it ran. Some paleontologists feel *Merychippus* was the first true equid of modern type.

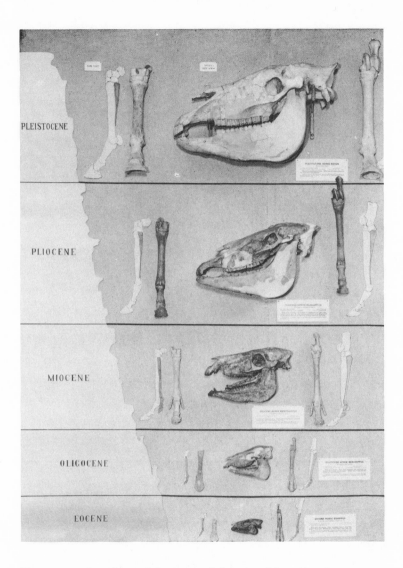

Changes in the physical features of the equid line that became to-day's *Equus* can be seen here. As the Cenozoic era passed through successive epochs, the horse developed longer bones in its legs, lost its side toes, and grew a larger head and jaw with better teeth for grazing.

Still, another 10 million years passed before a fully one-toed horse, *Pliohippus*, appeared in the late Miocene. And that much time again went by before *Equus* finally could be identified at the start of the Pleistocene, approximately 2,000,000 B.C.

Equus spread rather quickly through North and South America. It also crossed to Asia, presumably over the Bering Sea between Alaska and Siberia via the land bridges that may have risen and sunk several times during the Pleistocene — or were exposed when successive ice ages froze much of the world's water and lowered the level of the oceans several hundred feet. The last such bridge disappeared only about 14,000 years ago. In a relatively short time, geologically speaking, the *Equidae* penetrated into all of the Old World except isolated Australia.

The dispersion of the genus *Equus* also saw the evolution of its four modern subgenera. Each established itself in, and adapted to, a different area. The zebras thrived in southern and eastern Africa, the true asses in northern Africa. The Asiatic asses ranged northwest from Arabia to Europe and eastward as far as China. The horses generally stayed north, wandering freely from Mongolia westward as far as France and Spain. In some places the territory of one subgenus overlapped that of another, but it appears the subgenera did not interbreed. Here is a puzzle for the chromosome specialists to work on.

Another puzzle is why, after flourishing for some

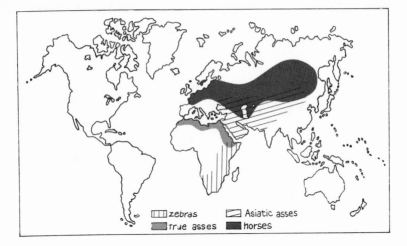

The distribution of the four equid subgenera, 10,000 or so years ago, shows approximately where each established its own Old World territory.

35 million years in America, equids died out there as recently as about 10,000 B.C. Many theories have been advanced to explain this — perhaps some kind of climatic crisis, the appearance of a deadly new parasite, the hunting prowess of Indian tribesmen — but the mystery remains. At least we are sure that the modern horse descended from the New World *Equus* by way of the Old World.

During most of the Pleistocene, wild horses roamed at will across the world's largest land mass. From western Europe to eastern Asia they found grass, water, and freedom to keep increasing until their herds numbered in the thousands. If winter brought cold, these hardy animals endured it or mi-

37

grated south. If predators came near, the wild horse had sharp eyes to see them, keen nostrils to sniff them out, and powerful legs to carry it to safety.

Most of the time, that is. Equids are among the fastest animals on earth. The zebra and Asiatic wild ass have been clocked at 40 miles per hour, and some racehorses can approach 50 m.p.h. within 80 yards. Modern horses have cleared heights of more than 8 feet. The small Pleistocene horse would have been almost as swift, almost as agile. But the modern lion also can hit 50 m.p.h. in one burst; the Cape hunting dog of South Africa can do 45 and the hyena, 40. So a Pleistocene predator could catch a weak or aged horse, or a foal, if it got close enough. And wild horses, like other animals, were also prey to various parasites, some of which carried diseases that could wipe out a whole herd.

Gradually, the horses established broad ranges, where separate types developed. Like people living in, say, Africa and China, each type tended to become distinct from the others. We have no way of knowing how or when that happened, how many different types evolved, or which ones survived to the start of the Recent epoch.

The lack of certain knowledge has led paleontologists to come up with a spectrum of theories about Pleistocene horses. At one end, some think that no less than eight types developed, each of which gave rise to a different type of domestic horse. At the other end, some feel that only one type

— the Przhevalsky — survived to become the ancestor of all domestic horses.

The truth probably lies somewhere in between. On fossil evidence, at least two horse types existed at the same time during some part of the Pleistocene. One was big and rather specialized in its physical characteristics. The other was medium sized and less differentiated. The large type died out, perhaps because it could not adapt to the extreme conditions of the glacial periods that occurred several times in the Pleistocene and later. (The last ice age ended only about 12,000 years ago, and we may be heading into another one.)

Each such period began with a worldwide drop in temperature, quite likely caused by changes in the angle of the earth's axis and thus the amount of sunlight received at different seasons. As the temperature fell, Arctic cold slowly spread over much of the Northern Hemisphere. In one period, ice up to two miles thick covered most of Europe. Many kinds of plants were frozen out, and animals had to migrate or adapt to year-round winter. Luckily, the coldest periods ended soon enough to let many animals return to where they had been before. But the large Pleistocene horse apparently didn't make it.

Two distinct types emerged from the smaller horse and survived to modern times. One was the Przhevalsky of Asia. The other was the lesser known tarpan, the wild horse of the southern Russian grassland. Not much bigger than a pony, but

39

The extinct tarpan probably looked a lot like this. Smaller and lighter than the Przhevalsky, it had a similar mane and dark stripe on the back.

strongly muscled, the tarpan was lighter and less chunky than the Przhevalsky. Its head was short, its ears small and pointed. Its coat was a light gray. But it had some features like a Przhevalsky's, including a black stripe along the back and a mane that stood up straight. Its winter coat was very pale, almost white. The tarpan must have been the wild white horse that the Greek historian Herodotus, some 500 years before Christ, described as living in marshland beside a river in what is now the Russian Ukraine.

Human beings too had evolved into much our present form by Pleistocene times. Like other mammals, we progressed very slowly over millions of years. But tremendous changes lay ahead. We now were moving toward a vast leap forward. Early people still got most of their food by hunting other animals, killing them, and eating their raw flesh. But their near future held such accomplishments as tools, fire, the wheel, agriculture, the weaving of clothes, and the building of houses.

Human evolution since the Pleistocene has produced the whole interlocked complex we call civilization. What it has done to the other animals in the world is something else.

Early humans probably left horses pretty much alone. Horses could easily outrun them, and humans could not kill them at a distance. They might trap one with luck. Or they might ambush one and throw rocks at it. The usual result of that would be only a tired throwing arm, but sometimes it was a feast of horseflesh.

By the time the Recent epoch began, humans had learned that horses and other ungulates could be killed in satisfactory numbers by stampeding them to the edge of a cliff, then over it. The bones of something like 10,000 horses have been found at one spot in France, apparently used by hunters for generations. That would have been roughly 15,000 years ago, not too long before the disappearance of equids in America.

Europe was home not only to wild horses, but to a variety of other animals, from reindeer and mammoth to hippopotamus and African elephant, that humans could hunt for food. To get it, they competed with wolves, bears, lions, and other predators. Some of these now have been extinct in Europe for a long time. But we know they existed there by their bones — and because people made pictures of them. Many were drawn, engraved, or painted on the walls of caves, notably in southern France and northern Spain. Others were carved in miniature on horn, bone, or ivory.

Early cave pictures are simple outlines, but later ones show that the artists had learned by experience and could produce works of high quality. Using two or more colors, a skilled painter could achieve a three-dimensional effect. Some paintings show animals running, leaping, fighting, alone and in groups. Some are so lifelike that they tempt observers to try to identify individual species. Equally realistic pictures were not created again for thousands of years.

How did primitive people achieve this? Equally important, why? Today painters paint partly for their own satisfaction and partly because they hope others will admire the results and even want to buy them. Cave artists certainly did not expect financial gain. Indeed, their paintings were done in such dark, hard-to-reach places that most people, it seems, were not supposed to see them. These artists painted from memory on a rough rock wall or ceiling, perhaps in a space so small that they could not

42

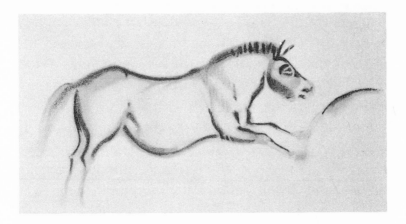

Yesterday's horse or today's? This lifelike painting of a horse very similar to a Przhevalsky was made on the dark inner wall of Font-de-Gaume, a cave in southern France. It probably is about 15,000 years old. In the same cave are realistic pictures of other modern mammals — wolves, reindeer, bison, wild cattle, rhinoceros — and wooly mammoths, now extinct.

stand erect, and they would have to work by the light of a flickering torch or a crude oil lamp and hurry to finish before the light gave out. No artist today would work under such conditions. Why did the cave painters do it?

A likely answer is that their paintings were thought to have magical powers. By creating a likeness of a horse out of thin air, so to speak, the artist seemed (to the primitive mind) to take possession of a vital part of the living animal. When those favored to share the creating went out to hunt horses, they would have some degree of control over them. In simplest terms, the painting would bring the hunters luck.

Horses were frequent subjects for cave art. They were pictured, time and again, with Przhevalsky (or tarpan) characteristics — heavy head and thick neck, bristling mane, back stripe, even the mealy nose. Seeing the skill with which they were depicted, it is just a bit hard to think they were admired only for their edibility.

But the time came when people stopped hunting horses and began domesticating them. That followed one of the great discoveries in human history — namely, that certain kinds of food plants could be sown, harvested, and replanted year after year. People now had a reliable source of regular nourishment, and they settled down where they could cultivate it. This was first done, it appears, along the rivers of the Near East, perhaps 12,000 years ago.

Once settled, people realized that certain wild animals could be made to contribute to their new life-style. Dogs already had come on the scene through the taming of wolves, perhaps as early as 15,000 B.C., to help track and hunt down game. Sheep and goats, first domesticated somewhere around 10,000 B.C., furnished wool for clothing and meat for the table. Cattle gave meat and milk. Pigs further diversified the diet.

Not until these five animals had been tamed did humans think about the horse, which of course was larger than the others, fleeter of foot, and found only in certain areas. One area was the Ukraine. Wild

44

horses, presumably tarpans, fed on the tall grass there, and roughly about 3500 B.C. the local herders saw that they could be caught and kept to provide meat, milk, and hides. That seems to have been the start of horse domestication. Gradually, the domestication of the horse spread east into Asia and west into Europe. And so *Equus*, the fiercely independent spirit of the open spaces, was tamed like lesser animals to become both property and servant.

Still, there was a difference between owning a dog or a cow and being the master of a horse. That fact was to have a profound impact on human progress.

The difference was grasped in Mesopotamia (today's Iraq), believed to be the birthplace of the wheel. When crude carts were developed, people harnessed animals to pull them — slow-pacing oxen . or the relatively small wild asses called onagers. After centuries of this practice, someone decided to try horses instead. They proved much faster than oxen, much stronger than onagers — in short, ideal for pulling wheeled vehicles.

Thus was born the horse's role in war. Carts became chariots, and fiery steeds took them into battle. The first time foot soldiers faced a war chariot — a rushing platform between two wheels, with a heavily armed man atop — must have been a dramatic meeting. The soldiers surely couldn't believe their eyes. This outlandish thing sweeping down on them was *real*? But indeed it was, and the army that had horse-drawn chariots was likely to win any battle it entered, unless the other side had them too.

The wild horses that had survived the glacial period were no bigger than ponies. Now the owners of domesticated horses began feeding them well to keep them strong and swift in battle. The same feeding, continued over generations, gradually made the animals bigger. Once that fact sank in, owners could experiment with selective breeding to make their horses taller, stronger, faster, or anything else thought desirable.

Greater size led to the final, most important step: riding the animals. Wild horses were too small for that. They also were nervous, inclined to bolt, and driven to frenzy by any strange weight on their backs — all qualities that would make any prospective rider think twice. Still, the time came when some brave soul managed to mount a horse, was thrown, climbed aboard again, was thrown again, and kept at it until at last the horse accepted this new relationship.

No one knows when it first happened, or where. It had happened in Egypt, at least, before about 1350 B.C., the date of a tomb where diggers unearthed the wooden figures of a horse and its rider. If in Egypt, then surely in other places.

When people learned to ride, they entered a new world. They could look down on other people, literally and figuratively. They could travel faster and farther than people on foot. They could go into

46

battle with speed and flexibility that not even a charioteer could match. The horse gave its rider a kind of power people had never known.

When a whole people could share that power, they became almost irresistible in war. Tribes and nations that had lived quietly for centuries, tending their crops and flocks, acquired horses and turned aggressive. Possession of horses made conquerors of the ancient Egyptians and Assyrians, the later Romans and Chinese, the hordes of Attila the Hun and Genghiz Khan, the Spaniards who subdued the New World, and the victorious forces of kings, chieftains, and gun-toting rebels. Not until the start of World War I in 1914 was the horse finally outmoded on the battlefield by gasoline-powered trucks, tanks, and armored cars.

The same thing happened in daily life. Horses pulled every kind of wheeled vehicle and carried every kind of rider. Without them, civilization would have advanced very differently. Here again it took the gasoline engine to end our dependence on the horse.

For thousands of years, horses have been a more intimate part of human life than any other domestic animal. One measure of their role is the uncounted number of horse paintings, sculptures, and other figures that have been produced since prehistoric times. Another is the early tabu against eating horseflesh, based on the horse's value in war. Horses became for many peoples a form of wealth.

In some cultures, it long was the custom when a chief died to bury him with one or more of his favorite mounts. (Such graves, sometimes holding dozens of horse skeletons, have been discovered all the way from the Ukraine across Asia to the Altai Mountains of Siberia.) Horses figure in myths and legends that go back before recorded history. Statues of men on horseback may be seen in most of the world's major cities.

For something like a hundred million years, the evolution of horses and humans moved like slow, slow trains on long, parallel tracks. Then the tracks joined. From that day on, horses helped decide the whole course of human progress.

Meanwhile, what was happening to the original wild horses that had made it all possible? In two words: slow death.

This was not apparent for a long time. Wild horses ran free in Europe and Asia for thousands of years after the first ones were tamed. But domestication itself meant the eventual end of the tarpans and the Przhevalskys.

A domestic horse, one that a person owned, fed, and cared for, was something valuable, something to be guarded. That became increasingly clear as specialized types were bred for particular tasks. A herd of wild horses in the vicinity could persuade domestic animals to run away. One wild stallion could carry off a dozen good mares. Then the owner would lose the fruits of years of labor and have to start over.

No sensible person would tolerate that. He might go after the wild horses with any available weapon or catch some of them and add them to the domestic herd. Again, he might fence the land to keep the wild horses out and the tame horses in. That also would cut the wild ones off from sources of food and water. Whatever the solution, the wild horses were the losers.

More important in the long run was the steady growth of human population. When civilization in Europe was limited to the northern rim of the Mediterranean Sea, there was plenty of room for animals to the north and east. But as central and eastern Europe began to get populated, horses had to move along or die. Some moved, then died anyway.

The same thing was going on in other parts of the world, and the result was a steady drop in the number of all equids. For example, the exotically marked South African zebra called a quagga became extinct in 1883, when the last one died in a European zoo.

By about that time the tarpan also became extinct. By the 1700s it had been reduced to limited areas of the Ukraine, but survived by hiding amid tall grass or reeds by day and coming out at night to graze. A German naturalist, S. G. Gmelin, visited the Ukraine in 1769 to observe tarpans and to kill a few for study. Local peasants gladly helped him round them up: Tarpans had been raiding their farms, gobbling up hay stored for the winter, carrying off occasional domestic mares. Such destruction led to frequent tarpan hunts in the area, which in turn hastened the animals' final disappearance.

Today, the only known tarpan remains are two skulls, one with its skeleton, in Soviet institutes. Gmelin's notes are among our few good sources on tarpan looks and behavior. Some zoologists who consider the tarpan and the Przhevalsky horse to be subspecies of a single species — that is, closely related but physically distinct and occupying different ranges — honor Gmelin by calling the tarpan *Equus przewalskii gmelini.*

The tarpan may well have been the ancestor of some domesticated horses still found in rural areas of eastern Europe, for example, the Polish *konik* and the *hutsul* of Hungary's Carpathian Mountains. Both of these are relatively small, not much bigger than ponies. They carry such tarpan markings as the black mane and tail, and their coats normally turn almost white in winter. But the relationship seems impossible to prove.

Since the tarpan's extinction, the Hellabrunn Zoo at Munich, West Germany, has conducted the novel experiment of trying to "re-create" it. Domestic horses have been chosen for physical characteristics as close as possible to what is known of the tarpan's and are then bred. The offspring, again hand-picked, have been bred further. Over several generations, a small, gray horse has been developed that seems to maintain its "tarpan" looks without further tampering. Some even have been sent to other zoos.

As for the Przhevalsky, it survived longer than the tarpan by going even farther away from people. Its once great numbers steadily reduced, its range lost bit by bit, it became an animal in hiding. John Bell, a Scottish doctor in the service of Tsar Peter the Great, traveled from Russia to China in 1719–1722, and his account of the trip includes the first known mention of the Przhevalsky in Western writing. He saw wild horses and termed them "the most watchful creatures alive. One of them waits always on the heights, to give warning to the rest; and, upon the least approach of danger, runs to the herd . . . upon which all of them fly away, like so many deer." Nonetheless, he saw native Kalmyks "ride in among them, well mounted on swift horses, and kill them with broad lances. Their flesh they esteem excellent food; and use their skins to sleep upon."

Lance attacks were bad enough, but guns, when the Asian tribesmen got them, were worse. By the time the horses had retreated into the arid zones of Mongolia and Sinkiang, they risked being shot on sight. Such spottings inevitably grew fewer. So far as the outside world knew, wild horses had died out by the second half of the nineteenth century.

Then in 1878 the Russian explorer Przhevalsky arrived at the border post of Zaisan, near the western edge of Sinkiang, and acquired the hide and skull of an animal shot in the vicinity. It was first thought they might belong to a feral horse or a wild ass, but they proved to be from an "extinct" species — *Equus przewalskii*. The last wild horse still lived.

THE EXPLORER

Nicolai M. Przhevalsky discovered the last wild horse, the animal that has given his own name a permanent place in the language of science, almost by accident. It happened when he was after bigger game — the chance to become the first European of his day to reach the hidden land of Tibet, high in the mighty Himalaya Mountains, and enter its capital, the "forbidden city" of Lhasa.

We have called him "the Russian explorer." Actually, few people outside Russia (and probably not many inside) know that Przhevalsky was one of the most important discoverers of the nineteenth century. He lived at a time when Europeans had penetrated most of the rest of the inhabited globe — the Americas, Australia, Africa, the South Seas — leav-

53

ing only one major area to beckon the brave. That was the wild, forbidding, landlocked expanse of central Asia. And there Przhevalsky chose to spend the best part of eighteen years, nearly a third of his life.

His exploits won him world fame, medals, honors, promotions, money, and the personal friendship of two tsars. But after his death his achievements were overshadowed by the march of great events, especially the revolution that tore tsarist Russia apart and remade it in the Communist mold. Today, in most of the world, even his name is scarcely remembered.

Yet his accomplishments were outstanding. He planned and led five major expeditions, totaling nearly 19,000 miles on horseback, camelback, muleback, and, when necessary, his own two feet. Setting out from various points along the long, winding border of Asiatic Russia, he made his way generally southward into the rugged emptiness of Mongolia and western China, an area of crumpled mountains and desolate deserts nearly as big as the contiguous United States. Most places he and his few companions went to were sparsely populated, and the people were often hostile to foreigners. Much of the area had been closed to outsiders for centuries.

Przhevalsky's wanderings took him to places no other European had ever seen, and some that had last been visited by Marco Polo, the famed Venetian traveler, some six centuries before. He surveyed and mapped thousands of miles of strange terrain. He made detailed observations on temperatures, altitudes, and winds. He discovered at least eight mountain ranges. He made invaluable collections of mammals, birds, reptiles, fishes, and plants, many of them new to European scientists. Discoveries that bear his name include not only the horse but also a gerbil (*Brachiones przewalskii*), a lizard (*Eremias przewalskii*), a lemming (*Eremiomys przewalskii*), a carp (*Schizopygopsis przewalskii*), and several plant species. He also found a wild camel, which for some reason is *not* named for him.

High amid the peaks of western China, Przhevalsky investigated the beginnings of China's two mightiest rivers, the Huang Ho and the Yangtze Kiang, each longer than the Mississippi. He located the mysterious "lost" lake called Lop Nor, which had "disappeared" after being shown on Chinese maps for two thousand years. Thanks to Przhevalsky, geographers learned that the northern border of the Tibetan plateau was 200 miles north of where they had thought it was. He penetrated Tibet to a point only 160 miles from Lhasa, where he was turned back at gunpoint. It was one of his few failures.

Russia in Przhevalsky's day had a clearcut foreign policy in Asia: Annex all the territory you can and extend your influence as far as possible. The process really had begun two centuries before, when

Russian pioneers made their way from the Ural Mountains (the traditional boundary between Europe and Asia) all the way across the largely unpeopled breadth of Siberia to the Pacific Ocean. Annexation of most of Siberia followed. The final far-eastern chunk, along the north bank of the Amur River and the area south to Korea, was wrested from a weak Chinese government in 1858–1860.

During this period, Russia had occupied, one after another, a series of once independent states running southeast from the Black Sea past the Caucasus and the Caspian Sea deep into the steppes of western Asia. That thrust extended the Russian Empire to the borders of Persia (now Iran) and Afghanistan, a performance watched with growing alarm by the British forces then entrenched in India. The British Empire, too, was busy trading and colonizing wherever it could, and London had plans to move north from India into Tibet and the Asian heartland. The two great powers thus were on a collision course in that part of the world; feelings between them ran high for decades; and open war almost broke out on several occasions. The tension ended only when both governments finally agreed to keep hands off central Asia and turned their attention to other matters.

Nicolai Przhevalsky was well aware of his tsar's interest in Tibet, western China, and Mongolia. He was quite willing to further that interest whenever he could, particularly since he was an officer in the imperial army, and the government financed most of his travels. But he was essentially a loner, self-reliant, impatient with interference, reluctant to get involved with others unless he had no choice. Like other great explorers, he responded to the unknown as to a personal challenge.

Like other explorers, too, Przhevalsky put up with delays, inconveniences, and dangers that might have stopped less self-confident men. He survived for months on boiled tea, barley meal, and whatever game he could shoot. Sometimes he went weeks without being able to wash his face. When he lacked money to hire help, he himself did such chores as loading pack camels and gathering dried animal dung as fuel for cooking. If his scientific instruments were damaged or stolen, he improvised. For example, after an aneroid barometer for measuring altitudes was broken, he went right on measuring by noting the temperatures at which water boiled (the greater the altitude, the lower the boiling point).

With all his positive qualities, Przhevalsky was a contradictory person. When not gorging on game, he liked nothing better than gobbling jam or candy and other sweets. He loved nature and the solitude of the wilderness, but killed animals so single-mindedly that often their carcasses had to be left to rot. He became a father figure to younger men, but never had (nor apparently wanted) children of his own.

Nicolai Przhevalsky's good looks dominate this photo taken about 1875, when he was in his mid-30s. It comes from the collection of the Zoological Institute of the Soviet Academy of Sciences in Leningrad, U.S.S.R.

He was devoted to a few individuals but had a low opinion of the human race and its civilization. The notes he kept, and his letters home, are dotted with comments critical of humanity. St. Petersburg,

Russia's capital during his lifetime (renamed Leningrad when the capital was shifted to Moscow after the 1917 revolution), literally made him sick with its noise, dirt, and swarming people.

Przhevalsky's impatience with any viewpoint but his own may have reflected his confidence in his ability to surmount obstacles. It also may have been a family trait. His mother, one biographer says, was "good looking and of strong character — characteristics inherited by Nicolai Mikhailovich."

About the good looks there is little question. Tall and well built, blue-eyed, somewhat dark-skinned, with black hair worn fairly long and a sweeping mustache, Przhevalsky as a young man was slim and dashing in his military uniform. Thanks to his love for rich food, he grew heavier as the years passed. In a photograph taken when he was forty-seven and a major general, he bears a marked resemblance to the heavyset dictator Joseph Stalin, who ruled the Soviet Union before and during World War II. Still, Przhevalsky remained an imposing figure always.

As for the strong character, he went after what he wanted and usually got it. Inevitably, he offended some people. In his teens he was considered standoffish. As a young officer, he was respected but not regarded as "a good comrade." One biographer sums it up: "The young man annoyed others with his self-assurance."

Considering what he faced in central Asia in the 1870s and 1880s, this trait wasn't necessarily bad. An explorer in those times, in that area, needed all the self-assurance he could get.

Nicolai Przhevalsky was born April 12, 1839, in the Smolensk *oblast* (region) of western Russia. Tsar Nicholas I occupied the throne at St. Petersburg. Smolensk today is a city of some 225,000 people on the Dnepr River about 240 miles west of Moscow. In Przhevalsky's time it was the small provincial capital of a largely flat, partly forested area.

Mikhail Przhevalsky, Nicolai's father, was descended from Ukrainian Cossacks and enjoyed the status of "squire" and a family coat of arms. He had served in the Russian army, then retired at the age of thirty-two. Though in poor health and almost penniless, he managed to win the hand of Yelena Karetnikova, daughter of a moderately prosperous landowner.

Mikhail and Yelena had three sons, Nicolai, Vladimir (1840), and Yevgeni (1843). They built themselves a house and called it Otradnoye (Aw-TRAHD-nah-yeh), which means "joyful." Then in 1846 Mikhail died.

Fortunately, Yelena inherited a share in her father's property. The family had more land than money, but the three Przhevalsky boys were brought up as gentlemen. All three did well: Nicolai became a general, Vladimir a judge, Yevgeni a mathematician.

A sturdy woman named Olga Makaryevna (Mah-KAH-rah-yev-nah) kept house for the family and doubled as the boys' nurse. Her fairy tales and stories of adventure sent them to sleep night after night and helped inspire Nicolai's later dreams of exploring unknown places. He loved her dearly. Indeed, she and his mother were the only women he ever loved.

The boys had a freewheeling sort of childhood. There were almost no books in the house, so they played by the hour, indoors and out, together or with the servants' children. Yelena's brother Pavel came to live with them and became the boys' tutor. He taught them to read and write, started them learning French, and showed them how to relax between lessons at his own favorite sport, hunting small animals and birds. Nicolai began with toy guns, went on to bows and arrows, and at twelve was given his father's shotgun. Later he acknowledged that hunting also taught him to appreciate trees and flowers, rocks and streams — in short, nature.

When they were old enough Nicolai and Vladimir were enrolled in the Smolensk *gimnazia*, or advanced school. They didn't like it much. The teachers tried to instill facts by endless repetition and kept discipline through severe beatings.

Nicolai was not a very good student, but he had a

photographic memory that could store whole pages of problems and answers until he needed them. Years later, he could recall everything on a textbook page just by being given the page number.

In 1854, when he was fifteen, his mother remarried. Meanwhile, Russia had gotten embroiled in the Crimean War. Ranged against her were Turkey, Great Britain, and France. The last two sent forces to besiege the Russian naval base of Sevastopol on the Crimean peninsula in the Black Sea. The siege was on when Przhevalsky graduated from school in 1855. Afire with patriotism, he volunteered for the army and at seventeen was made an officer cadet.

Unfortunately for his dreams of glory, Sevastopol had surrendered by then. Russia had lost the war. Tsar Nicholas had died and had been succeeded by his son, Alexander II. Instead of a heroic future, Nicolai faced years of routine peacetime service in isolated, boring garrison towns.

Depressed by the prospect, he began finding an escape by reading books about travel and adventure. Soon he was thinking about becoming an explorer in Africa or Asia. He read of the African exploits of such noted Englishmen as David Livingstone and Sir Samuel Baker and dreamed of

At right. Twice as wide as the United States, the Russian Empire in Przhevalsky's day (as now) straddled two continents. Przhevalsky needed months to travel — over dust and mud in summer, snow and ice in winter — to the frontier points where his actual explorations of unknown Asia could get under way.

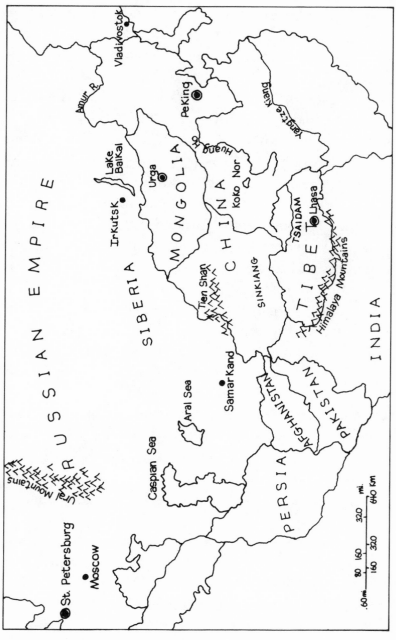

rushing off to join them. But his practical mind told him that Asia was a much better bet.

The best way to get there was by becoming an officer. Accordingly, Przhevalsky decided to try for the Academy of the General Staff in St. Petersburg. He had had far too little schooling to qualify, but he refused to let that stop him. Studying up to sixteen hours a day for a full year, he passed the tough entrance examination and entered a life of dedicated learning. Military subjects that an explorer could utilize — geography, surveying, and the like — were augmented by extensive reading in history, botany, and zoology. He even found time to bring in a little money by gambling at cards.

He also began his writing career. His first effort was an unpaid magazine article titled (what else?) "Memoirs of a Sportsman." Then he made a survey of all the information available on the distant area of the Amur River in eastern Siberia, newly acquired from China. He did this as part of his academic work, but the paper reached the Imperial Geographic Society and so impressed that body that he was elected to membership.

Przhevalsky never graduated from the academy. Instead, he and others in his class were offered officers' commissions if they would go on active duty in Poland, where a rebellion against Russian domination had broken out. Przhevalsky went, was made a lieutenant, saw only brief service — his nearest approach ever to actual battle — and returned to peacetime duty. Soon he was teaching history and geography at an army school in Warsaw.

He enjoyed working with younger men and made a good teacher. But by now his own eyes were fixed on Asia. When he felt he was ready, he asked for a transfer from Poland.

In 1866 he got great news: He was being assigned to the same Amur River district on which he had written his dissertation. It would take him nearly 6000 miles away. He would have to leave his family and Otradnoye for perhaps years. He could hardly wait.

In January 1867, after kissing his mother and nurse goodby, Przhevalsky was on his way to the Far East.

The Amur River district in 1867 was to Russia much what the land beyond the Mississippi was to the United States: the untamed frontier. Rough and unmapped, it had attracted only a scattering of hunters, trappers, and traders in the centuries of Chinese dominion. When St. Petersburg took over, settlers were forcibly recruited in other parts of Siberia and shipped east. Many of them were previously exiled criminals; some were given former prostitutes as wives. During this time, construction began on a big new seaport near the Korean border. It was named Vladivostok, which, appropriately, means "Ruler of the East."

Young Lieutenant Przhevalsky arrived in the district after months of travel from St. Petersburg by rail, horse-drawn sledge, steamboat (across Lake Baikal), and horses procured at relay posts. He had an extensive program to follow. It included reporting on Russian troops in the area, gathering information on the native population, making maps, collecting animal and plant specimens, and surveying the living conditions of the new Russian settlers.

During his two years' duty, Przhevalsky spent about as much time on his own pursuits as he did on official assignments. He traversed part of the Amur River by rowboat, made his way through dense forests to a remote lake and spent weeks there observing nature, took part in a foray against Chinese brigands, won thousands of rubles gambling in the frontier outpost of Nikolayevsk. But he also gathered specimens of more than 300 bird species, amassed a variety of statistics, and reported in typical Przhevalsky language that the Amur district struck him as "one slop-pit (of course I mean people, not nature) where everything low and disgusting is poured off from the whole of Russia."

His immediate superiors were not happy with such frank comments, but his overall results were very well received. He was promoted to captain and, once back in St. Petersburg, he arranged to publish a book on his experiences. (It was dedicated "To Dear Mother." Przhevalsky was then thirty years old.) The book had some success, and the author found himself a minor celebrity. He was invited to lecture on the Far East at the Geographical Society. Then he sought and received from that semigovernmental body a promise of partial funding for an expedition of his own into central Asia. At last his dreams seemed on the verge of coming true.

The army and the War Ministry also got involved in his plans. The British were moving from their Indian base into Burma, perhaps with some idea of pushing north from there into Tibet, and the Russian policy-makers felt that Przhevalsky's proposal might serve the cause of diplomacy as well as that of science. They too agreed to help finance him. Thus encouraged, he got down to making detailed preparations and lining up personnel, equipment, and supplies. In 1870 he was ready to go.

This time he planned to take three years and visit regions almost unknown in the West. His targets included the Gobi, the great desert of Mongolia, the middle reaches of China's Huang Ho or Yellow River, the Ordos and Ala Shan deserts of northern China, the mountainous western province of Kansu and its isolated, gemlike Koko Nor ("Blue Lake"). There also was the possibility of a southward journey to Tibet, which would give the British something to think about. Among Przhevalsky's scientific duties would be surveying, mapping, recording altitudes and temperatures, and collecting plants and animals.

Przhevalsky would not, of course, be the first human being in most of these places, nor necessarily the first European. Many peoples had lived in the Asian heartland. The majority were nomads who raised horses for hunting or for raiding more settled cultures. The mounted warriors who left the deepest imprint on history were those of Genghiz Khan, the Mongol chieftain born in the latter 1100s. Genghiz led his fierce tribesmen first against China. (An early chronicle says it was on that march that he staged a wild horse hunt and fell off his own horse when some wild ones suddenly crossed in front of him.) Then he turned westward, raiding and setting up an empire that eventually reached all the way to Hungary and Poland. Some of his followers and their descendants, known as the Golden Horde, ruled Russia for two centuries.

Marco Polo crossed Asia in the late 1200s, following ancient caravan routes. His reports gave western Europeans their first good picture of the area. Later, other travelers occasionally penetrated the heartland. But much of Mongolia and western China, Tibet in particular, remained a blank in Western knowledge from Marco Polo's day to Przhevalsky's.

The full story of Przhevalsky's five Asiatic expeditions is too long to tell here. In any case, we are concerned mainly with the first two and the start of the third, with emphasis on the wild horse. Here are some highlights:

Przhevalsky's first expedition (1870–1873) began, like his "dry run" to the Amur, in Irkutsk, Siberia.

Instead of heading east, though, he turned south to Kyakhta on the Mongolian border. Kyakhta had been for more than a century the only entry for trade between the Russian and Chinese empires. From it a caravan road ran southeast across Mongolia roughly a thousand miles to Peking. Przhevalsky had been told to take this route in order to secure a Chinese passport for his further travels.

He left Kyakhta with a young assistant, Mikhail Pyltsov, and a setter named Faust. They traveled some 200 miles in a boxlike, two-wheeled cart drawn by camels ("The shaking in this kind of car baffles description," he noted) as far as Mongolia's capital, Urga.* Then they struck out across the Gobi with a camel caravan, often walking ahead to shoot at game. The Gobi is one of the world's biggest deserts, a giant arc a thousand miles long and up to 600 miles wide, a good deal of it not sand but bare rock. It makes for slow travel.

After they reached Peking and got the passports, Przhevalsky bought riding horses and pack camels, supplies and food. Then they took an experimental run into a largely unexplored section of southeastern Mongolia, circling back to the trading center of Kalgan, northwest of Peking. Przhevalsky surveyed

*This was the Russian and European name. The Mongol name was Bogdo-Kuren ("Sacred Encampment"); it was the main center of the Buddhist faith outside Tibet. When Mongolia became independent after World War I, helped by the new Communist regime in Russia, the capital was renamed Ulan Bator ("Red Hero").

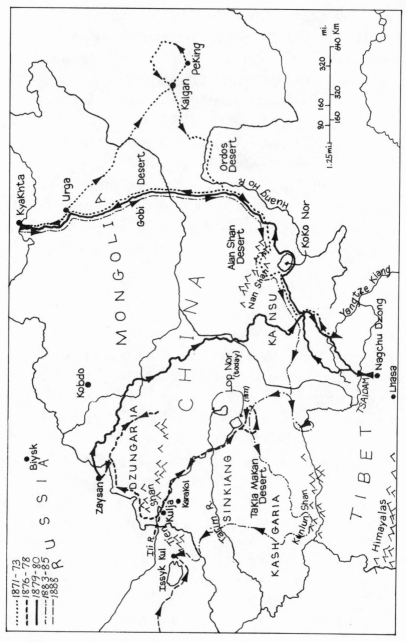

their route; they shot and observed birds; and the leader made notes.

One note was on the Mongol horses they saw. "They are rather under the average height, their legs and neck thick, their heads large, their coat long and shaggy. They possess wonderful powers of endurance, remaining out in the open in the extreme cold, and contenting themselves with the scanty herbage. . . . They will live where other horses would perish in a month's time."

He was describing domestic animals, but he could almost as well have been talking about the wild ones he would see later on.

In Kalgan the party added two Cossacks to help with everyday chores and headed westward. After a while they came to the Huang Ho, which loops across China from Tibet to the Yellow Sea. North of the river they entered well-watered mountains where Przhevalsky noted a wealth of trees and shrubs, with flowers of many hues "now intermingling in pleasant variety, now grouped in masses of color. But the sight is still more brilliant in the early morning when the first rays of the sun sparkle on the dewdrops hanging on every petal." After such poetic thoughts, it is a jolt (though hardly a surprise) to read complaints about the difficulty of hunting

At left. Przhevalsky's four complete expeditions and his unfinished fifth one can be followed on this map of the Asian heartland. Only his main routes appear; he also made many side trips to view local geographic features.

deer and gazelle among the rugged cliffs and chasms. "Sport in these mountains hardly repays the trouble."

When he was through sightseeing, Przhevalsky led the way back down to the Huang Ho and the Ordos Desert, which lies in a great bend of the river. The Ordos offered nearly 200 miles of barren sand hillocks. Then came the Ala Shan, an even less alluring desert. It lies on a high plateau, west of the Huang Ho, with expanses of sand where almost nothing grows. Przhevalsky wrote of its "deathlike solitude."

The expedition covered 120 miles of the Ala Shan, with wells spaced up to 30 miles apart and virtually no fodder for their animals. On the far side they reached the district capital, Ting-yüan-Ying, and became friendly with its prince. Przhevalsky was able to spend two weeks hunting the *koko-yamaan* or blue goat in the nearby mountains. Then he found that his money was almost used up and they would have to return to Kalgan.

They set out in late fall. Pyltsov, the assistant, was laid low nine days with typhoid fever. Moving cautiously on, they were hit by blizzards. Then it turned so cold that there was a real question whether they would get through. When they ate meat, the fat froze solid on their hands. Nor did they always eat meat. One day they managed 23 miles in a snowstorm. After pitching camp, they could find no fuel, not even cattle dung. So, Prezhevalsky

Camels and native herders have accompanied many European expeditions into Asia. This group was sent out to hunt animals for the German dealer Carl Hagenbeck, but others much like it traveled with Przhevalsky.

wrote, "We were obliged to cut up a saddle in order to boil a little tea" — their entire meal. They could go on just so long at that rate.

They staggered into Kalgan as 1872 began. They had lost twelve camels and eleven horses on that terrible march. Yet Przhevalsky was still full of energy. He sent off a collection of specimens. Then he hastened to Peking, where the Russian ambassador helped him get more money from home.

Again in Kalgan, Przhevalsky got replacements for the first two Cossacks, who had grown homesick, and led the way back along the Huang Ho to the Ala Shan and Ting-yüan-ying. More desert stretched ahead, but beyond came the high, rainy mountains of Kansu province. Up there lived the Tanguts, a rather primitive people related in language and culture to the Tibetans. There, too, was Koko Nor, the lake Przhevalsky greatly desired to reach. The way was uncertain and he had no guide, but, by luck, he reached Ting-yüan-ying just as a caravan of pious Tanguts was about to start for a Buddhist lamasery near Koko Nor. He arranged to go with them.

The Tanguts were glad to have well-armed Europeans along, for their route lay through country infested with Moslem rebels called Tungans. (China in those days was afflicted with frequent rebellions.) Przhevalsky was not worried by the Tungans. Still, as the caravan moved ahead, he admitted that they were good at burning villages and destroying farms. And they had killed a lot of people, throwing the bodies where they pleased. One day the party stopped to drink tea made with water from a desert well. Afterward, they found a rotting corpse at the bottom.

They crossed the Great Wall of China, in this distant region only a dilapidated mud structure, and entered Kansu. Soon they began climbing into cool, verdant mountains. These were the Nan Shan ("Northern Mountains"), first of the many ranges lying between them and Tibet.

74

Here Przhevalsky and Pyltsov left their companions to explore the trackless forest. They were in a botanist's paradise. Przhevalsky noted a red-barked birch tree new to Europe and described for the first time the true medicinal rhubarb, which grows at 10,000 feet and higher. At 13,000 feet he came on a small, silent lake and "remained more than an hour on its shore absorbed in reverie." In a few weeks the two men collected 324 species of plants and 124 of birds.

This, of course, was not getting them to Koko Nor, so they moved to lower ground and a lamasery called Chobsen, where they had left some of their things on the way up. The place was jammed with troops, Tangut families, and livestock: An attack by hundreds of Tungans was expected at any time. Przhevalsky calmly pitched camp with Pyltsov and the Cossacks outside the lamasery walls. No attack came. Eventually, the Tanguts felt safe enough to bring out their animals, and Przhevalsky arranged to join a group of Mongols headed north toward Koko Nor.

The Chobsen episode contributed to his growing reputation among the primitive people of the area as a man of special powers. For example, he could cure people of fever (by dosing them with quinine), accurately predict a meteorite shower (which he knew was coming), conduct mystic rituals with strange instruments (actually being used for surveying).

When hundreds of Tungans refused to attack just four men, surely it meant that Przhevalsky was a great magician, possibly even a saint.

So they came to Koko Nor, a mountain lake of unusual beauty, 2300 square miles of dark blue salt water 10,500 feet high and surrounded by higher mountains — many of them, in October, topped with snow. Przhevalsky walked down to the water's edge and stood looking at the panorama in "complete delight." "The dream of my life was accomplished," he wrote, "and the object of the expedition gained!" But his trip was not over yet.

On the shores of Koko Nor he found a Mongol camp, where, to his utter surprise, the Tibetan ambassador to China had stopped en route home from Peking. They talked (through an interpreter), and the ambassador assured the Russian that he would be welcome in Lhasa. That amounted to an invitation, and Przhevalsky accepted at once. Lhasa was a prize far greater than Koko Nor. But once again he had a financial problem. His remaining funds would take the party about 500 miles and back. That was only half way to Lhasa. Still, it was worth a try.

Guides led him from Koko Nor westward, then south through the Nan Shan into the Tsaidam basin, which occupies the northeastern section of the Tibetan plateau. Tsaidam is cut off to the south by the massive Kunlun Shan, last major mountain system before the king of them all, the Himalayas. Toward the Kunluns the party now headed.

It was November. Tsaidam was cold, barren, and racked by northwest gales. The ground was so rough and salty that the camels and even Faust the setter could barely walk on it. Wild camels and even wild horses were said to be in the area, but they saw almost no animals except a new species of pheasant.

Climbing through driving snowstorms, they came onto a high plateau whose average height was close to 14,000 feet. Oxygen starvation hit the whole party. Camels died and men shook with nausea. Still they kept going. In December they became the first Russians to penetrate the northern border of Tibet.

Przhevalsky celebrated by going out to shoot yaks. They provided meat and surprisingly good sport. "Wild yak are still attractive," he noted approvingly, "because this animal sometimes charges the hunter."

Apart from such treats, the trip offered little but hardship. The thermometer never got above freezing. Wolves followed them, stealing everything from yak carcasses to a rifle complete with cartridges. Food ran low, then lower.

In January, struggling through blinding dust storms, they reached the upper Yangtze Kiang, and there Przhevalsky accepted the inevitable. He had about enough money left to buy one sheep. Lhasa still lay a hard month's march to the south. Kyakhta and Irkutsk were many hundreds of miles to the north. That way they now had to go.

At least it was a physical relief to leave Tibet.

The goal Przhevalsky never reached: near Lhasa, capital of Tibet, the huge Potala palace rises above the rocky plain. It was long Buddhism's holy of holies, where the Dalai Lama held court. In it were, among other things, the Dalai's treasury, the state prison, and a big monastery.

They got back to Tsaidam, then Koko Nor, then the Nan Shan in spring. Przhevalsky collected scores of flower specimens in the Kansu mountains. He also heard of a weird human-animal, or animal-human, unknown in Russia. The Tanguts called it *hung-guresu*. He was eager to see one, but never did.*

*This sounds like the creature now called the Yeti or Abominable Snowman, supposedly living in the Himalayas. When Przhevalsky reported on it, no one in St. Petersburg believed him. His request for further investigation was ignored, and his report was hidden away, and rediscovered only in the 1950s.

From Kansu they moved down into the Ala Shan Desert, then north toward the Gobi and Urga. Learning that Tungans had ruined most of the wells along the regular route, they gambled on a course no other Europeans had ever taken. It proved to be one of the worst experiences yet. The sun was like fire. Even in the shade, the ground was sometimes too hot to touch. Water ran low, and one sad day the heat killed Faust the setter. Przhevalsky wept as he buried him. The ordeal went on for the best part of 600 miles. Przhevalsky wrote: "This desert is so terrible that by comparison the deserts of northern Tibet may be called fruitful."

When they reached the Russian consulate at Urga, they had been more than six weeks crossing the Gobi. They were too weak to stand erect. But they had made it.

That first expedition cost 18,000 rubles and the lives of twenty-four horses and fifty-five camels. It was worth it. Przhevalsky had reached far places that other travelers had not even been able to get near. He had surveyed, mapped, recorded, and collected. Even though a good part of his time was given over to bird migrations and hunting, he wound up with more knowledge of central Asia than any European before him. On every count the expedition was a success.

Word of his feats preceded him to St. Petersburg and caught the imagination of the public. He arrived a conquering hero. The War Minister interviewed him on the details of the trip. The Imperial Geographic Society gave him a special medal. When his stuffed birds and mammals were put on display, Tsar Alexander II came to inspect them, then bought them for 10,000 rubles and donated them to the Academy of Science. Przhevalsky received a promotion to lieutenant colonel, with higher pay and a life pension. (Pyltsov also was promoted.) His exploits were written up in newspapers and magazines. Aristocrats invited him to dine. He was given a leave of absence to write a book about his Asian travels.

The book finished, Przhevalsky planned another expedition to the heartland. It would enter from the west, via Sinkiang, rather than through Mongolia. After crossing the steppes from European Russia, he would reach the fertile valley of the Ili River, which rises in the Chinese part of the range called Tien Shan ("Celestial Mountains") and flows westward into the Russian part. The valley then would lead his party into Sinkiang.*

Sinkiang covers nearly 650,000 square miles, a sixth of China. Landlocked and hard to reach, it is one of the world's most forbidding terrains. From north to south its surface is like a series of giant

*Sinkiang means "New Dominion," the name given it in the third century B.C. when it first came into Chinese hands. In the nineteenth century, Europeans called it Chinese Turkestan. It now is the Sinkiang Uighur Autonomous Region.

waves. From the Altai Mountains on the Siberian and Mongolian borders the land comes down to the Dzungarian basin (also called Dzungaria), partly desert but partly fertile, with good grass that feeds domestic livestock — and once fed Przhevalsky horses. Southward the land rises to the Tien Shan, then drops again to a second basin, the Tarim (also called Kashgaria). This is largely barren desert rimmed by occasional oases. From its southern border rears the high, rugged Kunlun Shan.

Przhevalsky wanted to angle southeast across the Tien Shan into the Tarim basin and its desolate Takla Makan Desert. In the eastern Takla Makan, almost lost to the outside world, he hoped to rediscover the fabled lake of Lop Nor. Then he would head south into the Altyn Tagh, first of the ranges that make up the Kunluns. For a while he proposed to go on through the Kunluns to the Himalayas, visit Tibet's capital, Lhasa, and proceed down into India and Burma. The Geographic Society prudently cut out the last part of the proposal but approved it as far as Lhasa, provided Przhevalsky could get there and back in two years.

Confident as always, Przhevalsky lined up new men, animals, and equipment and set his sights on Kulja, the main town of the Ili Valley. Actually Chinese (and properly called I-ning), Kulja and its vicinity had been occupied not long before by Russian troops. They were there "temporarily," St. Petersburg declared, "to keep order" after a

Moslem adventurer named Yakub Beg left Russia and took advantage of the Tungan uprising to proclaim his personal "Kingdom of Kashgaria" in southern Sinkiang. Russia was inclined to support Yakub Beg because of the embarrassment he caused China. But even as Przhevalsky's party approached, in the hot summer of 1876, a Chinese army was heading for Sinkiang to try to expel Yakub.

With an armed clash looming, Przhevalsky logically could have put off his trip. But St. Petersburg wanted him to go ahead, so much so that it won promises from both Peking and Yakub Beg that his party could proceed in safety. Proceed they did.

Przhevalsky's second expedition (1876–1878) left Kulja with twenty-four camels and four horses. Going up the valley of the Ili, they ate well on local mutton and fruit. Then they entered a well-watered plateau where game abounded. They stayed there three weeks, "hunting most of the time," and bagged some good skins, including two of the now very rare sheep *Ovis ammon poli*. This species is named for none other than Marco Polo, who first described its magnificent flaring horns (which may grow more than six feet long).

The party now descended into the Tarim basin. The ground grew dry and the vegetation became sparse. When they reached an oasis controlled by Yakub Beg, they soon were met by an armed guard

— ostensibly to serve as guide, but actually to keep watch on their activities for Ya'ub.

Thus restricted, they made their way across the Takla Makan, central Asia's largest sand desert. This is a truly forsaken region, uninhabited except near the few oases, so dry that almost nothing can grow and the soil, thick with salt, is heaped by the prevailing northeast wind into miles of shifting dunes. "Dusty vapor," wrote Przhevalsky, fills the air like a fog."

They reached the shallow Tarim River, main watercourse of the Takla Makan, fed by glacial runoff from snowfields and glaciers in the surrounding mountains. It flows eastward into the driest part of the desert. As Przhevalsky's party followed it downstream, they came to an area of reeds and salt grass where the river grew even more shallow and began forming separate channels that ran parallel or vanished into the sand. What lay beyond?

What lay beyond was Lop Nor, a lake with a unique distinction: It lies farther from the ocean than any other lake on earth. The Chinese knew of it 2000 or more years ago and marked it on their maps. It long was thought to be the source of the Huang Ho. The river presumably ran underground from Lop Nor southeast to the mountains of Tibet, where it was believed somehow to surface in a high marshy area known, from its many springs, as the "Sea of Stars." This was indeed the actual origin of the aboveground Hoang Ho, but the underground connection with Lop Nor was unlikely.

Marco Polo passed near Lop Nor on his way to China, but apparently did not know it was there. No other outsider seemed sure about it. The Chinese tended to regard it as a place of mystery, better left alone. The old maps put it vaguely in the northern part of eastern Takla Makan, where it would have been formed as a catchment of the Tarim River. Since it had no surface outlet, its water logically would be salt.

Now, following the Tarim eastward, Przhevalsky noted a change in its direction to southeast, then almost south. And suddenly the water opened out ahead, stretching to the flat horizon. They had come on a lake.

Its edges were hard to be sure of. The going was muddy, the footing precarious. The constant haze blurred their vision. But gradually they reconnoitered the vicinity. They found a primitive people dwelling among the reeds, hunting and fishing for a living, and questioned them. Though Przhevalsky noted that this lake was roughly a hundred miles south of where Lop Nor was supposed to be, and further, that its water was fresh, the conclusion was inescapable: The old maps were wrong and this was indeed Lop Nor.

Their stay by the lake was interrupted by winter weather, which led Przhevalsky to seek a change of scene. The Altyn Tagh range awaited them, south across the desert, and its rocky peaks reportedly sheltered wild camels. The party, still escorted by Yakub Beg's men, thereupon headed south. Two discoveries resulted.

First, the distance to the base of the mountains was far less than expected. European geographers had placed them nearly 200 miles farther south. That meant 200 extra miles of mountains before reaching Lhasa — something Przhevalsky did not want to try in winter.

Second, the wild camels were few and far between. Przhevalsky spent six weeks looking for them, fighting wind, snow, and cold, and saw virtually no game larger than rabbits. Months later, he settled for three camel skins and a skull that he obtained from native hunters.

By February the party was back at Lop Nor, where the northward spring migration of millions of birds was beginning. Most of them belonged to only a few species of waterfowl, and Przhevalsky felt no compunction about shooting all he could. For a while the party ate twenty-four ducks a day, eight at each meal.

When that grew tiresome, they moved on — northward. The frequent windstorms, heavy with salt and dust, had killed off most of their camels. Przhevalsky did not feel he could reach Lhasa without fresh animals and good guides. The only thing to do was to retrace their steps up the Tarim and across the Tien Shan to Kulja, then start over.

They gratefully said farewell to their escorts at Yakub Beg's headquarters, and met Yakub himself for the first and only time. Przhevalsky was unimpressed with him. He felt sure the rebel's days were numbered. As it happened, Yakub died of a stroke a few weeks later, and Chinese soldiers began running wild in southern Sinkiang.

Kulja remained in Russian hands, and the party arrived there in August. Przhevalsky learned that he had been promoted to colonel, but otherwise the group was not in good shape. Heat, dirt, and insect bites had taken their toll. Worse, the leader himself had come down with an agonizing itch for which he could find no cure.

Despite everything, he got ready to head for Lhasa again. New Cossacks and camels were selected. So was a new route. To avoid the turmoil in Kashgaria, the party would swing north into the Dzungarian basin, then circle east and south.

They left Kulja not quite a year after the first departure. Again they had what seemed like plenty of everything, not forgetting marmalade and candy. They crossed the Tien Shan and came down into Dzungaria. It was unseasonably hot, and water proved scarce; the camels began to suffer; Przhevalsky's itch grew worse. Still they pressed on toward an oasis 300 miles away. When they reached it, nearly exhausted, Przhevalsky realized that he must have medical attention. For the second time the expedition turned back.

This time they headed not for Kulja but for Zaysan, a Russian frontier post 500 miles north. Zaysan had a small hospital and Przhevalsky at last got relief for his skin trouble as he awaited fresh orders from St. Petersburg.

When they came, they reflected new imperial concerns elsewhere. A Russo-Chinese war over the Ili Valley was threatening. Russia also was fighting Turkey again and seemed to be winning. But this was no time for even a full colonel to try to reach Lhasa. Instead, Przhevalsky was to go home and make new plans.

At home he was greeted by both bad news and good. The bad: His beloved mother had died of cancer while he was in Sinkiang. The good: His exploits were making him world famous. He received medals from Germany, France, and Great Britain. The noted German mapmaker August Petermann, whom Queen Victoria had named Britain's Geographer Royal, stated that Przhevalsky's discovery of Lop Nor "has the same geographical importance as the reaching of the North Pole or the crossing of Africa."

There was one sour note in the symphony of praise. The German geologist Baron von Richthofen, who knew something of Asia, disagreed politely but publicly. Thanks to Przhevalsky, he said, in a speech before a scientific meeting, "we find our knowledge of central Asia wonderfully extended, and our interest in it greatly excited. . . . We receive from the talented explorer comprehensive and suggestive conclusions on the animal and plant life. ... His travels [may well] compare with many of the most remarkable expeditions of modern times on African soil."

But Lop Nor, Von Richthofen stressed, always had been known as a salt lake in the northern part of the desert. If Przhevalsky had found a fresh-water lake south of there, it could not be Lop Nor. It *could* be a new lake created by a branch channel of the Tarim. In sum, the problem "requires more thorough investigation."

Przhevalsky naturally defended himself. He reminded Von Richthofen that Chinese information on the area was "misleading and inaccurate." He had seen no sign of a lake to the north. He had seen nothing to indicate that the Tarim had more than one main channel. He had found Lop Nor, period.

Von Richthofen remained unconvinced. Przhevalsky, after a second visit to the lake in 1885, repeated his earlier conclusion; indeed, he died believing it. Von Richthofen, who outlived him by seventeen years, remained unconvinced until *his* death.

The great Lop Nor argument was finally settled by Sven Hedin, a Swedish explorer in the Przhevalsky mold. He visited Lop Nor in 1895 and again in 1900. There was a lake right where Przhevalsky had said it was. But to the north, Hedin found the dry bed of a lake right where the Chinese (and Von Richthofen) had placed it. The existing lake was fresh, very shallow, and surrounded by flat, sandy terrain. Though the Tarim flowed into it, the flow was so slow that the river tended to clog up with silt and decayed vegetation. Also, the steady storms from the northeast would help choke it with sand. Then it would have to find a new channel — which, Hedin figured, would be the original one leading to the now dry lake bed. When that occurred, the original Lop Nor would refill and the present lake would dry up.

Hedin speculated that this had happened more than once. The lake had disappeared in one place and reappeared in another. He predicted it would happen again fairly soon. Sure enough, when he visited the area once more in 1928, river and lake had returned to their historic locations. Przhevalsky *and* Von Richthofen had been right about Lop Nor.*

Przhevalsky's third expedition (1879–1880) was planned as an all-out effort to go straight to Lhasa. In view of his government's continuing desire to beat the British to Tibet, he proposed a two-year trip with a hidden purpose. "Scientific explorations," he explained, "will mask the political aims of the expedition and deflect any suspicions of those hostile to us." His proposal was accepted.

Things were not yet quiet in Sinkiang. Chinese

*Still remote and isolated, the Lop Nor area has become the source of a rather different type of news. The Communist Chinese now use it as their main site for testing nuclear missiles.

soldiers were on the loose in Kashgaria, and Russia still clung to the Ili Valley despite strong Chinese protests. St. Petersburg nonetheless managed a safe-travel promise for Przhevalsky.

He planned to start from Zaysan, where he had ended his previous trip, and cross the upper Dzungarian basin. Then he would swing south, cross the western Gobi and the Nan Shan, and work his way through Tsaidam into Tibet. It meant going hundreds of miles out of the direct line, but it would avoid Kashgaria. Przhevalsky hired two young assistants, Fyodor Eklon and Vsevelod Roborovsky. The final group totaled fifteen men and twenty-three camels.

In Zaysan, something unexpected happened: Przhevalsky was presented with the skull and hide of a wild horse.

There is disagreement on the timing of this event. One good source says it was in 1878, at the end of his second expedition. Another good source says it was in 1879, at the start of the third. It is not clear whether he took the hide and skull to Russia himself or had them sent there.

In any case, the horse had been shot by native hunters in the Dzungarian Desert east of Zaysan and brought in to A. K. Tikhanov (TEE-kha-noff), master of the post there. Tikhanov gave the hide and skull to Przhevalsky. And the explorer, who had studied zoology and heard reports of wild horses in several places, felt sure the remains belonged to such an animal, most likely a tarpan.

When the skull and hide (with a wooly winter coat) reached the Zoological Museum of the Russian Academy of Sciences in St. Petersburg, they were taken over by I. S. Poliakov, the museum's curator. Careful and thorough, he determined that the remains came from a three-year-old animal. (Later researchers found it was younger, perhaps only about fifteen months.) He measured the teeth, jaws, eye sockets, and so on, and compared them with those of other equids. In 1881 he announced that this was a genuine wild horse, not a tarpan but a previously unknown type. The hide and skull, stuffed and mounted in a reasonably lifelike pose, went on display (and may be seen today in the Zoological Institute of the Soviet Academy of Sciences in Leningrad).

Poliakov's announcement created a great stir among scientists, and much argument. Some zoologists accepted his judgment. Others insisted that the wild horse was extinct and that Przhevalsky had acquired some other animal, probably a wild ass. Poliakov ignored the argument and named the horse *Equus przewalskii*.

The explorer himself had no doubts. For one reason, he actually saw wild horses as he was crossing Dzungaria in 1879. (They raced away before he could shoot one.) About 400 miles farther on, near a

Mongolian oasis called Gashun Nor, he saw two more small herds, each consisting of a stallion and several mares. One herd let him get within rifle shot, "but the animals caught my companion's scent at not less than a thousand yards [more than half a mile] and withdrew."

Przhevalsky was in Chinese territory, and Peking, despite earlier assurances, wanted him out. To gain time, he promised the authorities in one town that he would go off for six weeks of hunting, then return. Once away, he led his men straight for Tsaidam and Tibet. This ruse freed him from interference. It also cut him off from contact with the outside world. By the time the party reached Tibet, it was reported that Przhevalsky was lost, a Chinese prisoner — or dead.

Unaware of all that, he blazed a trail through previously unexplored terrain at altitudes of 14,000 feet and up. (For comparison, California's Mt. Whitney, highest peak in the contiguous United States, is 14,494 feet.) The land was bare and stony, the weather formidable. They could have been the first people in the area. When they came on such game as yaks and kulans, the animals showed no alarm. Shooting them was close to butchery.

But the game vanished, the snow fell heavily, and they slogged ahead sustained largely on hope. Every mile brought Lhasa closer. They came to the uppermost reaches of the Yangtze Kiang, flowing fast through gorges too deep to penetrate. They were attacked by nomadic bandits. They kept going.

At last they approached Nagchu Dzong, Tibet's northernmost outpost. There they were met by Tibetan soldiers. The expedition had come more than 2000 miles since leaving Zaysan, and Lhasa was just 160 more miles away. But the Tibetan government was panicky at their arrival. (One rumor was that the Russians wanted to kidnap Buddhism's holiest man, the Dalai Lama.) The soldiers forced them to stop and wait for official word from Lhasa.

The word came after eighteen days: They must leave Tibet at once. Przhevalsky, dejected, disgusted, and in no mood to battle the Tibetan militia, had to comply. Bartering for food, losing camels to sickness and cold, the party fought blizzards back to the Yangtze as 1880 began.

Conditions improved as they recrossed Tsaidam into the Nan Shan. There they picked up the route Przhevalsky had followed in 1873. He kept collecting plants, and had nearly 900 by the time they reached the border at Kyakhta. That wasn't exactly like becoming the first Russian in Lhasa, but it was better than nothing.

Przhevalsky returned to St. Petersburg and a welcome suitable for a hero who had been given up for dead. Medals, honors, and invitations showered down. Tsar Alexander II was assassinated in March 1881, but his son Alexander III was cordial to Przhevalsky. The explorer even was asked to the palace to describe his travels to the thirteen-year-old Tsarevich Nicholas II. The young prince was entranced.

When he could get away, Przhevalsky headed for a new estate he had purchased in the wildest part of Smolensk *oblast*. It was called Sloboda. Since it lacked a main house, he slept in the open and lived on game. Then he set about to have a proper house built, to be furnished with Asian trophies.

That year saw the dispute over the Ili Valley end. The Russians agreed to leave, and there was peace with China — temporarily.

Przhevalsky now began planning yet another expedition. Even before his house was half finished, he had mapped his route, won official support, and organized his party. Fyodor Eklon suddenly turned traitor: He got married. Przhevalsky replaced him with a young man named Pyotr Koslov who was to become not only his devoted assistant but his champion in later years. With Koslov, Roborovsky (who had been with him on his third trip), and eighteen other men, the explorer prepared to head south once again from Kyakhta.

Przhevalsky's fourth expedition (1883–1885) was basically designed to fill gaps left from earlier trips, particularly in the northern Tibetan mountains and the nearby Takla Makan Desert. Finding the source of the Huang Ho was a major goal. Reaching Lhasa was a minor one, if that.

The route from Kyakhta was familiar — across the

Gobi, past Koko Nor and through Tsaidam to the eastern Altyn Tagh. There they plunged into wilderness. Climbing steadily, they reached 16,000 feet before coming to a secluded plateau. There they found it — the fabled Sea of Stars whose springs join their waters to flow 3000 miles to the Chinese coast. They had crossed the Huang Ho repeatedly, lower down. Now they became possibly the first Europeans to see its birth.

Bitter weather pursued them at those heights. Even in June their camels' hooves were cut by jagged ice. Still they made their way from the Sea of Stars to the headwaters of the other great river, the Yangtze Kiang. They once again fought off attacks by hostile tribesmen. Then, safely back in Tsaidam, they turned west along the rim of the Kunlun Shan and began a new project: to find a practical route from north or west through the mountains to Tibet.

Winter came on, and the mountain passes were like Arctic wind tunnels. They tried one way, another, yet another. At nearly 12,000 feet they stumbled on a lake which, miraculously, was free of ice; Przhevalsky named it the Unfreezing Lake. Finally, they found the pass they wanted — the most direct way yet to move into Tibet from the direction of Russia.

Back on lower ground, they marched along the rim of the desert and came to Lop Nor on the side opposite to Przhevalsky's earlier visit. Then they bore west, skirting the mountains and stopping at ancient oases. They were harassed, though never attacked, by Chinese troops. From Khotan, the last oasis, they marched 500 miles north to the Russian border and the town of Karakol on the eastern shore of the Issyk Kul ("Dark Lake"). A few weeks more and they were in St. Petersburg.

The discoveries of those two years won Przhevalsky a promotion to the rank of major general, with more medals and other honors. He also was questioned officially on how he thought Russia would fare if war should break out with China. Przhevalsky offered his opinion that Russia could easily move into Kashgaria and take over the rest of Sinkiang — and the additional advice that it be done promptly, preferably by provoking the Chinese to declare war. The government noted his opinion but sensibly tabled his advice.

Back at Sloboda, he was happy for a time. Then his continuing distaste for European civilization made him restless again. His house was finished and suitably adorned with everything from a stuffed Tibetan bear to signed portraits of the Tsarevich Nicholas. But, even as he moved in, he was outlining a fifth expedition. It would retrace the last part of his fourth one, back to the Kunlun Shan, and then, perhaps as a final dramatic effort, drive once more for Lhasa.

His proposal was approved. The necessary ar-

Full of years and honors, Przhevalsky poses for his last portrait. It was taken in 1886, two years before his death. His body has thickened, his hair has lost its wave, but he still sports a substantial mustache.

rangements were made. In August 1888, the party left St. Petersburg for Moscow and points southeast.

Looking back, we can see bad omens for this expedition. Przhevalsky was in good general health but overweight and oddly lacking in mental energy. His old nurse, Makaryevna, fatally ill with a kidney ailment, died before he reached Moscow. The weather was wearingly hot as the party took a steamer down the Volga River and another across the Caspian Sea; Przhevalsky was seasick two days. They traveled to Samarkand on a new railroad, but from there to Karakol it was a jolting ride over poor roads. Przhevalsky grew very depressed. He told Roborovsky that if he survived this trip he would have to grow old with little to live for. It would be better, he said, to die in the arms of his men.

And so it came to pass. As they progressed toward Karakol, Przhevalsky decided to go hunting along the Chu River. Roborovsky went with him. The day was hot, and Przhevalsky stopped to drink from the river — over protests from his aide, who knew there was typhoid fever about. The next day, Przhevalsky felt ill. Three days later, when they camped on the southern shore of the Issyk Kul, he was feverish. A doctor came and moved him to the military hospital in Karakol. His condition grew steadily worse. He died the following night with his men around him. It was November 1, 1888. Nicolai Przhevalsky was forty-nine.

He was buried there by the lake, far from home but deep in the wild solitude he loved. He had wanted a simple coffin, but over the grave was erected a monument topped by a bronze eagle with a map of Asia at its feet; on the back, an olive branch, symbol of the peaceful conquest of science;

on the front, Przhevalsky's name and dates, and a replica of the Imperial Geographic Society medal reading, "To the first explorer of the nature of central Asia."

His last expedition was completed without him. It made no effort to reach Lhasa. Some of his successors, notably Pyotr Koslov, led other Asiatic explorations, and some reached Tibet. No Russian officer, however, got to Lhasa. Przhevalsky's goal was attained by British explorers (and later, of course, by Chinese troops).

Russia mourned Przhevalsky's loss and honored him in several ways. Karakol, where he had died, was renamed Przhevalsk. Studies of his animal and plant collections were published over a period of years; indeed, some of his botanical specimens have not been classified yet. A range in the Kunlun Shan that he had named The Mysterious was renamed, by the Geographic Society, Przhevalsky's Range. (The Chinese never accepted that.) In 1939 the Soviet government held a national observance of the one-hundredth anniversary of his birth, with publication of tributes to his bravery and patriotism. Though his house at Sloboda was burned down in World War II, the village of Sloboda was renamed Przhevalskoye in 1964.

Other countries gave scant attention to the man who probably contributed more than anyone else of his generation to the world's knowledge of central

Asia. If, indeed, his achievements have been pushed aside by later events, it still is ironic that his name lives on mainly because, among so many other things, he happened to discover the animal named *Equus przewalskii*.

THE RESCUERS

News of Przhevalsky's horse created at least as much interest among zoologists as his reports on lakes and mountains did among geographers. Here was a primeval, untamed animal — one that everyone thought was extinct — alive and roaming the "lost world" of central Asia. It was hard to believe in the up-to-date year 1881.

Looking back, it would be heartwarming to say that the first impulse of the civilized world was to try to rescue the Przhevalsky horse from oblivion. That effort did come later, but at the time there was more curiosity than concern. What did the horse look like? How was it put together? How did it compare with other equids? Was it in fact the surviving ancestor of the domestic horse?

101

Answers to all such questions depended on obtaining more wild horses, dead or alive. Russian explorers in Asia after Przhevalsky's death were urged to keep special watch for them. The first to report success were two brothers named Grum-Grzhmailo (Groom-Grzh-MY-lo), who managed to shoot four wild horses in Dzungaria in 1889–1890; three of the hides and skulls were sent to the Academy of Sciences and are still on display in Leningrad. Fortunately, the brothers also made fairly full notes on the behavior of the animals. Those notes have become our best source of information on how wild horses used to live.

Roborovsky and Koslov, Przhevalsky's former aides, led an expedition in 1895 that produced another hide and skull. Three more were secured during the 1890s. A Russian expert, A. A. Tikhomirov (Te-kha-ME-roff), examined all these remains and concluded that Poliakov had been right: *Equus przewalskii* was a sure-enough wild horse. That settled the question for just about everybody.

At the same time, zoos and animal collectors wanted to see the animal in the flesh. That meant organizing and financing expeditions designed to capture the horse alive.

A Russian again was the leader in this quest. His name was N. I. Assanov (Ah-SAHN-off) and he was a trader in the Siberian town of Biysk (BEESK), about 250 miles northwest of the point where the northern borders of Mongolia and Sinkiang meet. When he learned of the demand for Mongolian horses in Europe, he saw a chance to make some money.

In 1896 he came in contact with a Russian nobleman, Baron F. E. Falz-Fein, who bred various animals at Askania Nova, his estate near the Black Sea. Falz-Fein was interested in acquiring wild horses, partly for himself, partly to resell. He agreed to pay for an expedition to seek some in Mongolia. Assanov hired the necessary hunters and oversaw their activities. Before long they caught several foals by the method of chasing them until they could run no farther, than roping them.

This expedition took place in 1897, according to Falz-Fein, who wrote about the hunt thirty years later. He said all the captured foals died for lack of proper food, so he authorized another expedition. This time he ordered the foals to be caught by shooting their mothers. He planned to have domestic foster-mothers supply the nursing youngsters with milk. A domestic mare would do this sometimes if her own foal were killed and its hide placed on a wild foal to make the mare accept the latter as her own. This brutal system apparently worked. In 1899, Falz-Fein said, seven foals were taken and four of them survived the long, slow journey to Askania Nova.

D. A. Clemenz, a Russian archeologist who had been working in Mongolia and who helped bring Falz-Fein and Assanov together, wrote about the same event in 1903. He said no foals were caught in

1897, a year devoted to preparations. In 1898 the hunters took six foals; all died because the hunters tried to feed them on sheep's milk. In 1899, more foals were caught. Four survived and, after wintering in Biysk, were transported to Askania Nova in 1900. Clemenz's account agrees with Falz-Fein's generally, but was written a lot closer to the event. Therefore, 1900 is accepted as the year the first live Przhevalskys reached Europe.

Assanov continued to send hunters after foals and in 1900 he diplomatically presented a pair to Tsar Nicholas II (who as a boy had so admired Przhevalsky the explorer). The same year saw Assanov in possession of no less than fifty-one foals, a substantial fraction of the existing wild stock. Twenty-eight of those foals survived and went to Europe. How they got there is a story in itself.

It happened that the Duke of Bedford, owner of a noted English private zoo, also had grown eager for some Przhevalskys. He already had rescued the Père David deer from disappearance. This big, long-faced animal was a species unique to China when the French missionary-naturalist Père Armand David traveled in that country in 1865. The deer was extinct in the wild even then, but a herd was preserved in the imperial hunting park at Peking. Père David sent museum specimens to Paris, and the British ambassador to Peking sent a live pair to the London Zoo. A few more reached other zoos before 1900, the year the remaining deer in the imperial park were killed in the violence of the Boxer Rebellion. The Duke of Bedford apparently anticipated this. In 1898 he collected all the Père David deer in Europe and turned them loose in his park at Woburn Abbey. They flourished there, and zoos now have hundreds of their descendants.

Perhaps the duke felt it was up to him to save the Przhevalsky horse as well. Perhaps he just fancied having wild horses at Woburn Abbey. In any case, he commissioned Carl Hagenbeck of Hamburg, Germany, to get him some.

Hagenbeck was then the most famous animal dealer on earth. His agents and hunters ranged the far places for rare animals. He knew where to look for them, how to care for them after they were caught, and how to deliver them in good condition.* He asked and got top prices. He welcomed the duke's request and set out to fill it in his own way.

Years later, Hagenbeck wrote that in 1901 one of his best agents went to Russia and asked Baron Falz-Fein where his Przhevalskys had been captured. The baron refused to tell. The agent, Wilhelm Grieger, learned from other sources that they had been taken near Kobdo, a town in western Mongolia, then driven to Biysk. Grieger then went to St. Petersburg and arranged for himself and another agent to cross Siberia to Biysk by train and sledge.

*Hagenbeck also established a fine zoo in Hamburg that today is run by the fourth generation of his family.

Carl Hagenbeck in the early 1900s: his sharp eye for wild animals (and profits) supplied European and American zoos with exotic creatures previously almost unknown to the public, including giraffes, walruses, snow leopards, hippopotamuses, Siberian ibexes, elephant seals and others.

Hagenbeck described at length how the two agents went by camel from Biysk to Kobdo, a matter of more than 500 miles; organized and outfitted

Mongolian hunters; received the hunters' catch, fifty-one foals; and took them all the way to Hamburg, using the utmost care but arriving with only twenty-eight still alive.

The only thing wrong with this narrative was that the last part of it was pure fantasy. The two agents did go to Biysk, but they never went on to Kobdo, didn't hire hunters, and didn't head for Hamburg with a herd of fifty-one animals. Instead, they simply met the trader Assanov in Biysk, bought his twenty-eight young horses, and took them to Hamburg, with some domestic Mongolian mares to serve as wet nurses.

Grieger had purchased the foals in a straight business deal. Why Hagenbeck falsified the story later has never become clear. Incidentally, the deal outraged Baron Falz-Fein, who had expected to buy the twenty-eight foals himself.

As it was, the Duke of Bedford properly received twelve young horses, and the rest went to zoos in London, the Netherlands, France, Germany, and the United States. The following year, Hagenbeck brought eleven more foals to Hamburg. Five died, but the rest soon were placed in various zoos.

Meanwhile, Falz-Fein swallowed his outrage and imported six more wild horses, through Assanov, up to 1904. That year he also received one of the two horses originally given to the tsar. (The other had died.) His eleven animals, plus the thirty-four survivors of the two Hagenbeck shipments, totaled

Przhevalsky foals and Mongolian domestic wet-nurse mares crowd Carl Hagenbeck's zoo at Hamburg. They are part of the shipment brought from Mongolia in 1900 and distributed to the Duke of Bedford and other zoos.

forty-five. With a single Mongolian mare later sent to Askania Nova, that is the known roster of Przhevalsky horses taken alive from Asia: forty-six animals out of the multitudes that once roamed the open range.

The first horses to go on display in European and American zoos were, of course, quite a novelty. Many people hurried to see what they looked like. Often the result was something of a letdown. This wild horse, even under the exotic name *Equus przewalskii*, was really rather like a domestic one to look at. It certainly wasn't as arresting as a giraffe, a koala, or an orang-utan.

Few people realized then how near to extinction

108

the horse already was. The sightings of wild horses since Przhevalsky's day and the success of Assanov's hunters made it seem as though more could be obtained at any time. Yet even Assanov, as early as 1905, stopped trying to catch them because there were too few to repay the expense.

Thus, in a few years, the Przhevalsky horse might have completed the whole cycle: discovery, capture, display in zoos, and extinction. The main reason it did not meet this fate was that a few zoo directors, even then, encouraged captive animals to breed. Often enough the motive was sentimental: It seemed like a nice idea for an animal father and mother to have a baby, or several, so that the public could admire the happy family and enjoy the frolicking youngsters. Sometimes breeding was attempted out of curiosity, to see whether it could be done and what would result. After two or three failures, the effort usually was abandoned.

The average zoo did not even try to breed Przhevalsky horses. There were various reasons: It was too much trouble, or the personnel lacked experience with equids, or there wasn't enough room. Even if a Przhevalsky pair did produce offspring, there might be no place to put them.

The experience of New York's prestigious Bronx Zoo was typical. It received two Przhevalskys from Hagenbeck in 1902, then passed them along to the Cincinnati Zoo. In 1905 Hagenbeck sent two replacements, a stallion and a mare. Twelve wild

109

horses were born in the Bronx Zoo in the next twenty-four years — but for lack of space most of them were sent elsewhere, and the New York herd came to an end in 1951, when the last descendant of the original pair died at the age of twenty-six.

Of all the zoos that owned Przhevalsky horses, it was ultimately just five breeding stations in Europe and the United States that saved the wild horse. Four were established early, or fairly so. Askania Nova was first in 1900. Woburn Abbey followed in 1901. The third station developed in Germany, originally at Berlin, later at Munich. The fourth, and for years the most successful, was at Prague, Czechoslovakia. Its ranking was challenged after the Catskill Game Farm joined the group.

The experience of the five points to the difficulty of keeping a rare species alive, even in captivity. So little was known about caring for wild horses that most of the original imported ones died within a few years. Askania Nova and Berlin lost all their survivors in World War II, though Askania Nova was able to resume breeding later. Woburn Abbey let its herd die out in the 1950s.

The five stations are worth a quick visit each.

Askania Nova. This was a ranch-sized spread, 2100 acres of flat, fertile Ukrainian land, owned by a titled family of German origin. One of the Russian-born members, Fyodor, turned most of the place into an animal park late in the nineteenth century.

110

His intent was to bring in hoofed creatures from various places and let them run practically free. In 1896, for example, he imported some breeding pairs of African eland (largest of the world's antelopes), whose descendants eventually numbered more than fifty. He also experimented with hybrids, crossing a domestic horse with a zebra, for example. As the opportunity arose, he would sell off some of his stock.

Askania Nova was a logical station for Przhevalskys. Of the original ten received by Falz-Fein, however, eight died without breeding. The last two were mares. Luckily, the survivor of the tsar's pair was a healthy stallion. Named Waska, this was that very rare wild horse who would let himself be saddled and ridden. Apparently, it was possible to do so by keeping his legs tied at first, so that any violent movement made him fall down. Somewhere in Russia, there still must be a photograph of Waska, standing in profile, with a saddle and bridle on him — and a booted, fur-hatted man in the saddle, holding the reins very tight.*

Waska proved to be a successful sire and mated with both of the mares. From that start grew the Askania Nova stud, which survived both the Russian Revolution of 1917 and the chaotic period that followed. Askania Nova itself was taken over by the new Soviet government. Renamed the Askania

*An English horse trainer also broke a Przhevalsky to the saddle about 1904. He said it refused to canter and trotted at a shuffle.

111

Nova Experimental Station, it took orders from Moscow.* But its Przhevalsky herd continued to thrive, producing altogether thirty-seven pure-blooded foals up to 1940.

Some of those foals died young. Some were sold to European zoos, including four to Berlin. Then came World War II and the German invasion of the Ukraine. Two more horses were sent to Berlin, without permission. Every remaining pure-blooded Przhevalsky horse at Askania Nova perished in the subsequent fighting.

After the war, Askania Nova was reactivated very slowly. In 1949 a pure-blooded stallion, Orlik, was obtained from the Hellabrunn Zoo at Munich, but he had no company other than domestic mares until 1957. That year, a true Przhevalsky mare was brought in from Mongolia. Named Orlica III, she was the first of her kind to leave Asia in more than half a century — and probably the last ever. She and Orlik produced several foals; Orlik also sired others. The Askania Nova stud was back in business.

Woburn Abbey. Breeding began well there, but ended badly. It too was a nobleman's estate, set in the rolling countryside northwest of London. Part of the area was taken up by the family mansion, gardens, and outbuildings, but in 1901 there was room

*Today the park has been enlarged to 6570 acres (more than ten square miles). Its official name is Askania Nova Ukrainian Scientific-Research Cattle-Breeding Institute of the Steppe-Regions. And it specializes in "acclimatization, hybridization and domestication of mammals and birds."

for a herd of Père David deer, many other hoofed animals, and a dozen Przhevalskys. The Duke of Bedford did not obtain his horses specifically for breeding, but they soon began to do so. Thirteen foals are known to have been born at Woburn, and at least nine of them wound up at other zoos, including one in Australia. Beyond that, little is known. Woburn Abbey always was a private park. Complete Przhevalsky records apparently were not kept there, and all surviving records were destroyed after the last Woburn stallion died at twenty-six in 1955.

The German zoos. The Berlin Zoo, Germany's oldest, once was also the world's biggest — in population, anyway. Director Ludwig Heck's philosophy seemed to be, "If it's alive, we'll exhibit it." In 1901 the zoo gladly accepted two horses from the first Hagenbeck consignment. Unfortunately, they produced no offspring and for some years the zoo had no Przhevalskys at all. Then in 1926 it obtained a stallion from Askania Nova and the next year a mare. This pair had six foals, four of which lived until 1945, when the zoo and most of Berlin were demolished in the climactic battle of World War II.* That finished wild horse breeding in Berlin.

Two of the Berlin horses had spent most of the

*Before the war the Berlin Zoo had more than 4000 animals. Many died naturally during the long years of fighting, and many more from Allied bombs and the fires they caused. Eventually, when the city was besieged from both sides, the zoo had some of its ungulates killed for food and most of its carnivores and snakes put away as a public-safety measure. Just ninety-one animals were alive at war's end.

1930s at Hellabrunn, a good-sized zoo on the out-skirts of Munich in southern Germany. This was a loan between Lutz and Heinz Heck, sons of Ludwig and directors at that time of Berlin and Hellabrunn respectively. During the same period, three other Przhevalskys were acquired by Hellabrunn, and a good breeding herd was started there before the Berlin horses went home. Munich came through the war without major damage, so both Hellabrunn and its herd were able to keep up the good work.

Prague. Breeding of wild horses here began rela-tively late. There was no zoo yet in Prague in 1921–1923, when the Agricultural High School's re-search station took three Przhevalskys from the small zoo in Halle, near Leipzig, in what now is East Germany. With them came what is sometimes called the "Halle taint" — a phrase that needs a lit-tle explaining.

Originally, the zoo of the Halle Institute received a pair of pure-blooded foals from the first Hagen-beck consignment, with three Mongolian domestic mares as wet nurses. When the foals matured, the Halle Municipal Zoo undertook to research the rela-tionship between wild horses and other equids. The wild stallion was mated not only with the wild mare but also with the Mongolian domestic ones. The only male foal that resulted, in 1906, was from a domestic mare. In 1908 the first stallion died. After that the zoo mated his "tainted" half-breed son with pure-blooded mares only — but, so far as the purity

114

of the Halle line was concerned, the damage had been done. The half-breed son sired nine foals. Most of them died without offspring, but a stallion named Ali and a mare named Minka survived, were sent to Prague, and there carried on the "taint."

None of this may seem terribly important, but it has bothered some European zoologists and zookeepers very much. Concerned for the preservation of the Przhevalsky horse in its pure form, they protest that the Halle half-breed should not have been bred with true wild mares unless the offspring were clearly labeled "tainted." The opposed point of view maintains that even in the wild a Przhevalsky could easily have some domestic blood, making it just about impossible to tell whether any given individual carries only pure wild blood from a hundred or so generations back.

The argument in any case does not seem to have bothered the breeders at Prague. Ali and Minka, each with one-quarter domestic blood, were mated and produced five foals at the research station and at the Prague Zoo after that was opened in 1932. Ali died in 1934, but Minka had three more foals by a pure-blooded stallion acquired from the National Zoo in Washington, D.C. Two of these became parents. Three of Ali and Minka's foals also were bred to pure-blooded mates at Prague and elsewhere. The "Halle taint," in ever smaller fractions, thus was spread to several zoos.

Incidentally, the last of the Halle half-breed's

foals was a stallion named Jan, whose life in captivity proved more eventful than it would have been in the Dzungarian Desert. Born in 1922, he traveled to zoos in Rotterdam, Hellabrunn, Hamburg, London, and back to Hamburg. He survived the German bombing of Rotterdam in 1940 but lost an eye in the Allied bombing of Hamburg in 1942. He finally died in 1953, peacefully, at thirty-one years of age.

It was after the war that the Prague Zoo emerged as the world center of Przhevalsky breeding. Prague had not been seriously bombed or long fought over, and the horses came through unscathed. A notoriously intractable stallion named Uran, born in 1944, was a major addition. Starting in 1950, he sired thirty-five foals in fifteen years. Another potent sire, Bars (a son of Askania Nova's Mongolian-born Orlica III), joined the herd in 1965. Prague foals have gone to, among other places, Amsterdam, Antwerp, Budapest, Cologne, Havana, Leipzig, London, Moscow, Paris, and Warsaw.

Hellabrunn at the same time was having considerable success. Stallions from Askania Nova — and from London, descended from Woburn Abbey animals — were mated with mares of both the Askania Nova and Prague lines. Heinz Heck liked the former better (perhaps in part because it was free of the "Halle taint") and gradually let the Prague descendants die out. Hellabrunn's herd thereafter was consistently smaller than Prague's.

Catskill. This park covers 1300 acres on the west side of the Hudson River, about 140 miles north of New York City. It was opened in 1933 by German-born Roland Lindemann. His first interest was deer, several species of which were bred successfully. After the war he decided to branch out, and in 1956–1957 he bought ten horses from Hellabrunn. (Two years later he also added the younger Heinz Heck, nephew of Hellabrunn's director, to his staff.) From this solid nucleus, Catskill has come to rank with Prague as a major breeding station. Its foals, all of the Askania Nova line, are found in a growing number of zoos.

If the Przhevalsky horse has been snatched at the last possible moment from extinction, we can credit the concerned spirit of one zoo and one woman.

The zoo, of course, was Prague. It may have begun breeding wild horses almost casually, "because they were there," and the effort was hardly urgent so long as a fair number of horses presumably survived in Asia. But the destruction of so many in World War II, coupled with the capture of just one mare thereafter, made preservation of the species a crucial matter. Prague responded by singling out the wild horse — which was just one of several hundred animal species in the zoo — for special study and care. The horses in turn responded: By the late 1950s there were twenty of them at Prague, more than a third of all those in captivity and possibly as many as then existed in the wild.

Trying to get other zoos equally involved, Prague in 1959 played host to a four-day symposium of talks and discussions on the Przhevalsky. This was a first in the history of wild animal management. Scientists and zoo people came from both sides of the Iron Curtain. Most of the papers read were in Czech or Russian, but they pretty well summarized what was known of the history, nature, behavior, and care of wild horses. With translations as needed, everyone present learned something.

The meeting produced two constructive resolutions. The participants agreed, first, to take steps to preserve the Przhevalsky in its natural environment and, second, to cooperate to increase its numbers in captivity. The symposium's papers were printed in four languages in a book entitled *Equus* and widely distributed. Through the symposium, Prague gave the work of conservation a special kind of forward push.

The woman who added substantially to that push was a self-taught German zoologist, Dr. Erna Mohr. Her story is an unusual one. Sturdy and square-jawed, gentle and unassuming, chatty and companionable, she had a passion for hard work and a mind like a steel trap. Somehow, all at the same time, she carried on three separate careers — four, if you

118

Erna Mohr. The lady of many careers had time to befriend almost any kind of animal. This 1934 snapshot shows her cradling a baby donkey.

count her years of effort on behalf of the Przhevalsky horse.

Erna Mohr was born in Hamburg in 1894. Her father, a teacher, came from a farming family, and as a child she spent her summers on the farm. There she became close friends with the animals in the barnyard and the stable, and animals in turn became her life.

Like her father, she trained to be a teacher. Start-

119

ing at twenty, she taught first in elementary school and then in a school for retarded children. This career lasted twenty years.

Another career had begun even sooner, at eighteen, when she wangled a beginner's job in the section on ichthyology (the science of fishes) in the Hamburg Zoological Museum. Bit by bit she learned so much about that field that in 1934 she was named head of the museum's Section on Lower Vertebrates. That let her give up teaching. In time it led to probably the museum's most demanding job, head of the Section on Higher Vertebrates (birds and mammals).

As she became an expert on collecting and displaying animal specimens, she gradually contributed a good deal to general zoological knowledge — so much so that in 1950 she was awarded the honorary degree of Doctor of Zoology by the University of Munich. This would be remarkable anywhere, but was practically unheard of in Germany, where education traditionally was so rigidly structured that no one could even dream of an advanced degree without first doing years of university and graduate work.

In addition to teaching and her work in the museum, Dr. Mohr squeezed in yet a third career as a student of, and later a consultant to, the major zoos of Europe. She began, naturally enough, with Hamburg's Hagenbeck Zoo (and wrote a magazine article on the Hagenbeck family). From age twenty on,

120

she made systematic visits to every zoo she could reach, studying and photographing the animals. In 1917, having already published several papers on fishes, she brought out her first one on mammals. It dealt with the cracking sound that reindeer make when they run — a somewhat special subject, certainly, but one that revealed her amazing eye for details other people might overlook. She went on to write about muskrats and wombats, seals and wild swine, wolverines and muskoxen. The list of her published works finally reached eighty-four books and many articles.

In her spare time (what spare time?), Dr. Mohr kept various animals of her own for pleasure and study. She enjoyed listening to music and attending art exhibits. She translated a well-known French work, François Bourlière's *World of Mammals*, into German. She kept at her side what has been called a "bottomless handbag" stuffed with notes, pictures, and other items that could help start a conversation even with a total stranger.

She also carried on correspondence with zoo people, scientific people, and just people. One American woman who wrote unintroduced to ask her some animal questions received an answer that led to an exchange of not only letters and postcards but also, to the American's astonishment, Christmas presents — though they never met.

For all her natural warmth, Dr. Mohr was a hard-headed realist about the welfare of animals. She was

121

one of the first to recognize that conservation presented a scientific challenge, not just the chance to rear cute animal families behind bars. In the 1920s, when the wisent or European bison (related to the American species) was menaced with extinction, she helped found a society to protect the animal through planned breeding. As secretary of the society, she set up a system of keeping records on all the individual wisents in captivity, a system still working today.

The Przhevalsky horse seems to have touched a special spot in Dr. Mohr. She was fascinated by the individuals she saw in zoos, and moved to learn all she could about the species. This led her, she wrote later, "to get to know personally every wild horse in Europe." She visited every zoo that kept them, photographed them, and collected information about them. She even helped to arrange transfers between zoos and matings between horses. Her knowledge of the Przhevalsky became almost encyclopedic. Finally, she summed it up in a book, *Das Urwildpferd* ("The Original Wild Horse"), published in Germany in 1959. After her death, in 1968, the book was translated and brought out in England as *The Asiatic Wild Horse*. By any name, it is the basic source for every other book (including this one) that deals with Przhevalskys.

When *Das Urwildpferd* came out, Dr. Mohr included with it the first pedigree book of the Przhevalsky horse. Based on her own data, her book

122

Číslo karty Studbook number	Pohlaví Sex	Číslo evidenční Studbook name	Jméno House-name	Datum narození Date of birth	Otec Father	Matka Mother	Stanoviště Site
341.	M	Catskill 30	Rolo	31. VIII. 1965	171. Hell. 44 Bertold	138. Hell. 41 Rolanda	Catskill
392.	M	Catskill 40	Semori	30. V. 1968	150. Hell. 23 Severin	277. Catskill 14 Marianna	Catskill
408.	F	Catskill 42	Roxie	12. V. 1969	150. Hell. 23 Severin	267. Hell. 51 Roxane	Catskill
470.	M	Catskill 45	Rocky	21. V. 1970	150. Hell. 23 Severin	278. Hell. 52 Rocca	Catskill
505.	M	Catskill 51	Sirox	22. VI. 1971	157. Hell. 30 Sigi	267. Hell. 51 Roxane	Catskill
532.	M	Catskill 53	Burton	18. VI. 1972	171. Hell. 44 Bertold	228. Catskill 2 Bonnie Jaan	Catskill
535.	F	Catskill 55	Sevranna	30. VIII. 1972	150. Hell. 23 Severin	277. Catskill 14 Marianna	Catskill
566.	M	Catskill 59	Rolox	11. VIII. 1973	341. Catskill 30 Rolo	408. Catskill 42 Roxie	Catskill
558.	M	Catskill 61	Rolmar	20. VIII. 1973	341. Catskill 30 Rolo	277. Catskill 14 Marianna	Catskill

A page from the Przhevalsky studbook shows at a glance not only the name, birthdate, and parentage of the Catskill Game Farm's Rolox (No. 566) but also those of his father, Rolo (341), and mother, Roxie (408). The columns are identified first in Czech, since the studbook is published in Prague, then by English translations.

became the groundwork for a series of annual studbooks published by the Prague Zoo. Studbooks for wild animals were a fairly new idea at the time, patterned after the original one for Thoroughbred racehorses established in England in 1808, which had set forth the bloodlines of the Thoroughbreds and, over the years, saved buyers and breeders untold time, trouble, and money.

Erna Mohr produced her pedigree book not to enrich anyone — least of all herself — but because she wanted to give others the wealth of information she had amassed on individual horses. The book covers

228 of them, all those known to have been brought to Europe or born in captivity up to the end of 1958. Each horses's condensed biography may be read across nine columns of facts.

The method appears in the very first entry. Horse Number 1 (first column) is a male (second column) with the studbook name Kobdo 1 (third column), for the vicinity where he was caught, and then the "house name" Waska. (Very few of the early imported Przhevalskys received house names, but this was the same stallion that went to the tsar's stables and then to Askania Nova.) Next come the year of his birth and the date of his death, September 29, 1915. The columns for his parents are blank, but column nine records his various homes and when he arrived at them: 1899 Mongolia, 1900 Biysk, 1901 Tsarskoye Selo, May 28, 1904, Askania Nova.

A later entry shows how much information the book can offer. This is Number 121; female; studbook name, Washington 2 (she was the second foal born at the National Zoo in Washington, D.C.); house name, Roma. She was born April 25, 1932, and died July 16, 1949. Her father was Philadelphia 5; her mother, Philadelphia 6. From Washington she went in 1934 to Hamburg and in 1937 to Hellabrunn. Further on, among the horses born at Hellabrunn, we find Roma bearing foals there in 1938, 1942, and 1943. The third of these, Hellabrunn 19, was called Robert at Munich; when he went to Askania Nova in 1948 to become the new breeding king there, he was renamed Orlik.

Dr. Mohr's pedigree book was greeted with universal approval — almost. Some people objected to her including not only the stallion Ali from Halle, but also his half-breed father and all of Ali's descendants. The critics maintained that since those weren't pure-blooded Przhevalskys they didn't belong in the book. Dr. Mohr disagreed, and the "tainted" animals are still there.

The studbooks produced at the Prague Zoo follow Dr. Mohr's system in recording the changes in the Przhevalsky population in a given year. Information comes in from zoos and animal parks in response to a questionnaire and is recorded on individual cards in a master file. The owner of each horse gets a duplicate card. One side of each card lists the animal's dates and other data; the other side gives its ancestors and descendants to three generations. If the horse changes owners, its card goes along. When the horse dies, the card is returned to Prague and placed in the "dead" file.

The studbook is mailed out to interested persons and institutions all over the world. Part of their interest is to keep track of changes among the Przhevalskys. More important, the book shows at a glance where a stallion, a mare, or both might be obtained for breeding, and the bloodlines of each.

By and large, the 1959 symposium accomplished

quite a lot. It increased general knowledge of the Przhevalsky horse and the degree of awareness of the danger the species was in. As a result, more zoos began to exhibit wild horses, and some undertook to breed them. By 1962 the number in captivity had increased from fifty-seven (in 1959) to eighty-four.

In 1965 another symposium was held, this time at the East Berlin Zoo. Some twenty papers were read. Two resolutions were adopted that showed a long-range concern for trying to maintain the Przhevalsky in the wild. The first: "The government of the U.S.S.R. should be asked to ensure a special reservation for the Przhevalsky horse." The second: "The governments of Mongolia and China should be asked to do everything to preserve the wild horse in its original territory."

By 1973 there were 206 Przhevalskys in captivity. Besides the established breeding centers, four relatively new ones were functioning. Two were on opposite sides of the United States, in the Bronx Zoo and the San Diego Zoo (supplemented by the spacious San Diego Wild Animal Park). Two were in England, in Whipsnade Park near London (run by the London Zoo) and the privately owned Marwell Zoo near the English Channel.

A third symposium, the first in a non-Communist country, was held in 1976 at Munich's Hellabrunn Zoo. Its emphasis was on improving breeding practices and insuring the preservation of pure bloodlines. Among the conclusions: For correct identifi-

126

cation, every wild horse henceforth would be branded inside the thigh with the studbook number; for successful breeding, a zoo should keep at least two or three horses in an enclosure of at least 3000 square meters; the final aim of breeding should be to reestablish the Przhevalsky in Mongolia if a proper reserve can be created there; further symposiums would be held at least every four years. England's Marwell Zoo offered to serve as host in 1980.

Not the least valuable feature of a symposium is that it permits free interchange of ideas and information. The man or woman from Askania Nova, for example, sums up what he or she and the staff have learned in more than half a century of adapting wild equids to the Ukrainian steppe. The delegate from Budapest has some ideas on how to keep wild horses wild in captivity. The one from Brussels offers his or her belief that the main difference between domestic and wild horses is in "the angle of the lower part of the mandible [the lower jawbone] and the profile of the nose." The delegate from Chicago mutters to himself, or herself, "Oh, come on. If *that's* the only difference, why are we here?"

Other ways of sharing data exist, of course. Zoo personnel write a good many letters to one another, sometimes on day-to-day aspects of handling Przhevalskys. ("Our herd can use some new blood, so we're thinking of getting a horse or two from you. Do you think we should just turn them in with the others or keep them separated until they all get used to the idea?")

Specialized publications for zoos and animal scientists bring out Przhevalsky articles whenever they can get them. Thus, from Prague came the news that the health of the wild horses in that zoo, along with their breeding behavior, was markedly improved when they were shifted from a sheltered area by the Vltava River to a higher site where they would be exposed to the north wind. Also, the new quarters had rough, hard-surfaced ground that kept the animals' hooves from growing too long. This is far better than having to trim the hooves to shape — "which always involves some sort of risk, both to the men and the horses."

From San Diego a report was issued on a small feeding experiment that zookeepers, at least, found useful. The aim was to see whether ungulates that do not chew the cud (such as horses) digest the customary zoo diet more or less efficiently than those that do (such as cows). A Przhevalsky, a zebra, and two onagers were tested against a bison, two gazelles, and eight South American cameloids (llamas and such). All were fed the same mixed-grain pellets for two weeks. Result: The cud-chewers and the two onagers made slightly better use than the Przhevelsky and the zebra of the dry matter, crude protein, and cellulose in the pellets. Nonetheless, the researchers concluded that all the animals "can be fed a complete pelleted diet under zoo condi-

128

tions,"provided hay is added for coarse roughage to keep the animals from nibbling dirt, wood, and hair.

At Askania Nova they solved a different kind of problem. Several mares grazed on the steppe by day, then returned at night for water and supplementary feeding. When a new stallion was added to the group, he at once began chasing the mares away at night and refusing to come in himself. Soon he took off on a jaunt that covered more than 70 miles. After he was found, ten days later, the management looked at him severely and shipped him off to the Moscow Zoo.

There is a point on the globe where the line marking 45 degrees north of the equator crosses the line marking 94 degrees east of Greenwich. It lies in southwestern Mongolia, almost on the border of Sinkiang, and it is about as far from civilization as one can imagine. The landscape is dry, bare, and empty. The soil is brown, sandy, and strewn with rocks. Occasional rains cut sharp-edged stream channels where the water quickly sinks in and disappears. Underground moisture supports scattered plants, small and tough, that dot the dry watercourses like stitches on a seam.

Close to the meeting of 45 degrees north and 94 degrees east, a modest ridge rises perhaps 3000 feet above the plain. It lies mainly east and west, like the larger Altai Mountains to the north. Its flanks are eroded by steep gullies. It is not a ridge on which

This photograph shows the bare and desolate Mongolian terrain near Takhin Shara Nuru ridge, to which the Przhevalsky horse retreated when other ranges were lost.

anyone would want to spend much time, nor one where one would expect anything except possibly lizards to live.

Yet the Mongols call the ridge Takhin Shara Nuru, which means Yellow Horses Mountain. After the Przhevalsky horse was forced out of the rest of the world, this is the desolate place where it made its last stand.

Once, tribesmen saw herds of as many as 100 wild horses in the area. Now, none has been seen on or near Yellow Horses Mountain in years. None has been seen to the northwest, around Kobdo (now called Hovd). Nor have there been sightings where

130

Nicolai Przhevalsky traveled — Dzungaria, the Gobi, the Ala Shan. Are any left in the wild, anywhere?

Trustworthy information is hard to come by. Local people have been known to report sighting wild horses that actually turned out to be feral domestic animals, or kulans, or other wild asses.

In 1966 a Hungarian zoologist, Dr. Zoltan Kaszab, visited the Takhin Shara Nuru. To get there, he traveled more than 650 miles from Ulan Bator across open country with virtually no roads. He was in a specially equipped car with a Mongolian fellow scientist and a driver. They were moving along the

Along the desert border between southwestern Mongolia and Chinese Sinkiang lies the limited range, around the ridge called Takhin Shara Nuru, where Przhevalsky horses were last seen—and possibly may be seen again.

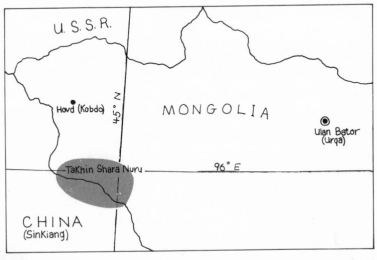

ridge when a group of eight animals suddenly galloped into view a mile or more ahead.

"Wild horses!" exclaimed the Mongolian scientist, who had seen some before. Kaszab, peering through binoculars, agreed with him.

At once they urged the driver to get them closer to the herd — and at once the animals headed away. The car was held to about 25 miles per hour on the rough terrain, so at that speed they kept up the chase for several miles. Then the herd vanished behind a slope of the ridge. Kaszab had been able to take two photographs of them. When those were developed, he could not be certain what they showed. However, the size of the hoofprints convinced him that they had been made by wild horses, not the smaller wild asses.

As on some other occasions, Kaszab's announcement led to a controversy. Once his photographs reached the Prague Zoo, they were examined with microscopic care by Dr. Jiri Volf, the zoo's curator of mammals and keeper of the Przhevalsky studbook. Dr. Volf concluded that Dr. Kaszab was mistaken. Those animals were not wild horses but kulans.

Both men stuck to their opinions. Sadly, there was no way to settle the disagreement. "Photographs don't lie" — but they may show different people different things.

In 1967 and 1968, the Biological Institute of Mongolia's Academy of Science sent out horse-hunting expeditions. They came back to report a total of five Przhevalskys in three separate sightings, plus accounts of a few others from herders. The matter rested there. At the time of this writing, the last presumably reliable sightings were in 1968.

A complete survey of the area would require helicopters. Even if more wild horses are spotted, it is highly unlikely that the species can survive in the wild. No animal can endure in an area too small for it to reproduce its kind. That is the case in Mongolia. Though the country is more than twice as big as Texas, five sixths of its area, some 500,000 square miles, is taken up by the almost uninhabitable Gobi. (By way of comparison, the Mojave Desert in southern California covers about 15,000 square miles.) And Mongolia supports close to 25,000,000 head of domestic livestock, more than 15 animals for every man, woman, and child. The majority are sheep and goats, but horses and cattle number nearly 2,500,000 each, and camels near 1,000,000. They all require food and water. To get those, the nomadic herders move their animals with the seasons. Wherever they go, they command the few natural water holes, the lakes and streams.

Under these conditions, might the wild horses still be protected? The Mongolian government banned hunting them in 1926, but even today that would not stop a herder from killing a horse for meat or to protect his own animals. China's government lately has urged herders to water their stock at artificial sources, such as wells, so that wild animals may use the natural sources. In both countries it sounds like too little, too late.

So the real hope of saving the wild horse remains with zoos. Though most of them continue to exhibit rather than breed, the major breeding stations now seem able to supply the demand from such zoos (at a price of $5000 or more per horse) and still increase their own herds. In early 1976, there were 243 Przhevalskys in more than 60 zoos and animal parks around the globe. There are more today. There will be still more tomorrow.

This success reflects three main facts.

First and most fortunate, these horses take well to life in captivity and are generally able to breed there. It is worth remembering that all the wild horses in zoos are descended from a few individuals brought from Asia in 1899–1902, plus the mare caught in 1947.

Second, breeders have learned by trial and error what conditions will best meet wild horses' natural needs, from chewy food to a place where a pregnant mare may have her foal in isolation.

Third, a great deal has been learned about keeping wild horses in optimum health. For example, many foals used to die within the first days or even hours after birth. It was found that they especially need vitamins at that time to help ward off infections. With vitamins and preventive medicines in the right dosages, the rate of foal deaths has been drastically cut.

Something else has been learned about Przhevalskys kept fenced in through generations: They run a strong risk of changing from a wild animal into one that is increasingly tame. The horse does not have to be broken and ridden (or made into a keeper's pet) for that to happen. All it has to do is live in surroundings where everything, good or bad, is provided for it by human beings. Food, shelter, exercise, medical attention — everything may be the best people can devise, but nothing is exactly what the horse would know in its wild habitat. Just as it evolved in nature under natural conditions, now it begins to be modified, bit by bit, under artificial conditions. This does not occur rapidly with every species, but it has been observed repeatedly in horses.

Sometimes the changes are psychological. For example, as the horse grows more and more at ease with people, it becomes less and less a true wild animal. Some changes are physical. For example, the teeth and jaws may gradually decrease in size, so that the horse loos more like a domestic animal than a Przhevalsky.

One other danger to captive horses is inbreeding. If a stallion sires foals by his own daughters, as happened particularly in the early days when so few horses were available, the possible result is the weakening of the stock. After some generations,

135

foals may be born with various physical and mental defects. (The bloodlines of any individual may be checked, of course, in the studbook.)

Inbreeding can be controlled as the number of Przhevalskys in captivity grows. Breeders can seek to rear only individuals that meet as closely as possible an agreed-on standard for the species. Animals that don't measure up could still be exhibited, but not bred. This would insure that only the best stock survived — a process that also applies in natural evolution.

As for overdomestication, concerned zookeepers are doing their best to keep their Przhevalskys in conditions approaching the wild. That is a great help in breeding. But it falls short of the real thing, where wild horses could stay wild forever. To achieve that, enough animals of high quality must be bred in captivity to fill the needs of the world's zoos and leave a substantial surplus. Then a place must be found where the surplus can run practically free.

One possibility is a reserve in Mongolia in the vicinity of the Takhin Shara Nuru. Hunting would have to be forbidden; grazing of domestic stock would have to be rigidly controlled; food and water for the Przhevalskys would have to be guaranteed. It sounds almost too good to be true. There are so many practical questions. How big would such a reserve have to be? How could it be kept supplied with whatever a wild horse might need? How could it all be fenced in and patrolled? Who would do the work? More important, who would pay for it?

Another possibility is a wild animal reserve that was established in 1939 by the Soviet government on a large island in the Aral Sea, a 25,000-square-mile body of water in the steppes east of the Caspian Sea. At least three kinds of animal have been set free there: the saiga (an Asiatic goat-antelope with an outsize nose), the kulan, and the Persian gazelle. All are ungulates, native to the area, and get along well together. If workable arrangements could be made between Russia and other countries, this might be a haven for wild horses as well.

So the rescuers of the Przhevalsky horse keep at their self-imposed task. One way or another, they mean to save it yet.

Compared with most wild animals, the Przhevalsky has received an exceptional amount of attention from zoologists and zookeepers. Much time, trouble, and money have gone into the international crusade to keep it alive. More will be required to return it to its natural environment and maintain it there.

Is one shaggy, standoffish equid worth all this?

Well, is any wild animal worth saving?

We human beings rarely thought so, at least until very recently. In the last four centuries we have allowed some 40 species of mammals and nearly 100 species of birds to vanish forever. At least 120 more species of mammals and 185 more species of birds are now in danger of disappearing. That leaves several thousand species to go, but the rate of extinction is speeding up.

The causes of this wholesale destruction are not hard to find. Some of the extinct species came to an end because they could not meet changing conditions, but the great majority have humans to thank. People have killed them off or brought predators (such as dogs) into their territories or destroyed their habitats by cutting down forests, draining swamps, and the like.

Most of the destruction was done, in a sense, by accident. People either paid no attention to what was happening or took it for granted that the animals would always be there. Once there was an excuse for that. Nicolai Przhevalsky could shoot ducks indefinitely at Lop Nor because he was just one hunter and there were millions of ducks. Even then, though, things were changing.

Around 1850, there were an estimated 9 billion passenger pigeons in North America. Then trigger-happy "sportsmen" began slaughtering them for fun and profit. Within 50 years they were virtually wiped out. The last lone female died in a zoo in 1914. With enough people shooting at what they thought was an inexhaustible supply of birds, the end of the species was just a matter of time.

Today there is less wanton killing in the developed countries, but people in Africa, Asia, and

South America still shoot animals for food or to protect their crops or herds. Obviously a balance must be worked out. People are not going to starve so that animals may live — but neither need animals be slaughtered just for human convenience.

In recent years, many countries have passed laws against killing endangered species or dealing in the live animals. International cooperation is growing. For example, the world's threatened polar bears are protected by a 1973 agreement among five Arctic nations: the United States, Canada, Denmark, Norway, and the Soviet Union. But some governments are lax about enforcing their own laws, and illegal poachers continue to supply rare animals to illegal dealers.

At the same time, animal habitats are steadily being lost to human uses. Timber is cut down. Open land is fenced. Natural and artificial lakes are enclosed to make reservoirs. Suburbs keep expanding. More and more space is preempted by factories, airfields, and superhighways.

For endangered species, the best hope now is zoos. They offer the one sure, safe place where wild animals can live and breed without fear of losing their lives to hunters or their homes to developers. Zoos now keep studbooks similar to the Przhevalsky's for more than 30 species of mammals and several birds, ranging from the brown hyena (Columbia Zoo, South Carolina) and the snow leopard (Brookfield Zoo, Chicago) to the okapi (Antwerp Zoo) and the stubby little Japanese serow (Tama Zoo, Tokyo). The very existence of a studbook shows that a species has been reduced to so few individuals that they can be counted and listed. Such a species has no chance to survive except in protected captivity.

Paradoxically, some animals are being bred *too* well in zoos. So far this applies mainly to the big cats: tigers, lions, leopards, and jaguars. All thrive in captivity, and all tend to have more litters there than in the wild. By a recent estimate, there were only some 200 Siberian tigers left in the wild, but more than 600 in captivity. Most zoos now have all the big cats they have room for and are using birth-control techniques to keep the population steady.

The Przhevalsky horse may seem less exotic than an okapi and a lot less fearsome than a Siberian tiger. Is it worth saving?

These are some of the arguments against and for:

— Thousands of animal and plant species have died out naturally in the long evolution of life on earth because they couldn't cope with changing conditions. If the Przhevalsky can't cope, too bad.

— A wild horse has practically no economic value, yet it costs thousands of dollars to breed, rear, feed, and care for just one of them. Why not apply that money to things human beings need?

— Even though domestic horses helped shape human history, machines have just about ended their usefulness. If people don't mind letting millions of domestic horses die off, why worry about a few wild ones?

On the other hand:

— If the Przhevalsky horse becomes extinct through human greed or indifference, that's hardly a natural process. Who are we to decree life or death for other forms of life?

— If there were no Przhevalskys at all, how much money actually would be saved for human needs? And what is meant by "human needs"? Don't they include the simple pleasure of looking at and studying a beautiful animal? Don't we want our children and our children's children to have that pleasure?

— Domestic horses were bred to serve humans. If machines can serve us better, the horses' existence, at least in great numbers, is no longer justified. But the wild horse is a unique creature that won its uniqueness by a hard and perilous climb that has lasted 60 million years. If it vanishes now, all that is lost forever.

Every biologist knows that all life on this earth is interlocked and interdependent. That includes humans. The extinction of even one species can have effects beyond imagination on all the rest. That includes humans.

The American naturalist Aldo Leopold said of the passing of the passenger pigeon, "There will always be pigeons in books and museums, but these are effigies and images, dead to all hardships and all delights. Book-pigeons cannot dive out of a cloud to make the deer run for cover. . . . They know no urge of seasons; they feel no kiss of sun, no lash of wind and weather; they live forever by not living at all."

The American astronomer Carl Sagan, noting that evolution on earth has taken too many random turns to be duplicated anywhere, said, "Never again, in any other place, will there be people or cows or grass."

Or wild horses, if we let them die.

BIBLIOGRAPHY

The following were the main volumes consulted by the author in researching this book. Also valuable were scientific and popular articles, encyclopedias, and other limited sources.

Bökönyi, Sándor *The Prjevalsky Horse*. London: Souvenir Press, 1974.

Bowden, C. R. *The Modern History of Mongolia*. New York: Praeger Publishers, 1968.

Crandall, Lee S. *Management of Wild Animals in Captivity*. Chicago and London: University of Chicago Press, 1964.

Dallin, David J. *The Rise of Russia in Asia*. New Haven, CT: Yale University Press, 1949.

Equus I. Prague: Zoologicka Zahrada Praha, 1961.

Equus II. East Berlin: Tierpark Berlin, 1967.

Fisher, James. *Wildlife in Danger*. New York: Viking Press, 1968.

Graves, Colin P. *Horses, Asses and Zebras in the Wild*. Hollywood, FL: Ralph Curtis Books, 1974.

Hagenbeck, Carl *Beasts and Men*. London: Longmans, Green, 1910.

Harper, Francis *Extinct and Vanishing Mammals of the Old World*. New York: American Committee for Wildlife Protection, 1945.

Hedin, Sven Anders *The Wandering Lake*. New York: E. P. Dutton, 1940.

International Zoo Yearbook, vols. 1, 3, 4, 5, 7, 14, 16. The Zoological Society of London. Various dates.

Mohr, Erna. *The Asiatic Wild Horse*. London: J.A. Allen, 1971.

Przhevalskii, Nicolai M. *Mongolia, the Tangut Country and the Solitudes of Northern Tibet*. London: Farnborough, Gregg, 1968.

————. *From Kulja, Across the Tian Shan to Lob-Nor*. New York: Greenwood Press, 1969.

Rayfield, Donald. *The Dream of Lhasa*. London: Elek Books, 1976.

Rudenko, Sergei I. *Frozen Tombs of Siberia*. Berkeley, CA: University of California Press, 1970.

Russki Biograficheskii Slovar', vol. 14. St. Petersburg: I. N. Skorokhodov, 1905.

Salensky, W. *Prjevalsky's Horse*. London: Hurst & Blackett, 1907.

Simpson, George G. *Horses*. New York: Oxford University Press, 1951.

Trippett, Frank. *The First Horsemen*. New York: Time-Life Books, 1974.

Vernadsky, George. *A History of Russia*. New Haven, CT: Yale University Press, 1961.

Zeuner, Friedrich E. *A History of Domesticated Animals*. New York: Harper & Row, 1964.